Human Rights Act Toolkit

The College of Law

2 NEW YORK ST.
MANCHESTER
M1 4HJ

TEL 01483 216708
e-mail: library.manchester@lawcol.co.uk

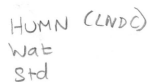

Jenny Watson was the last Chair of the Equal Opportunities Commission before the creation of the Equality and Human Rights Commission in 2007. She has previously worked in human rights organisations including the Human Rights Act Research Unit, Charter88 and Liberty, and now works with Global Partners and Associates.

Mitchell Woolf is a solicitor specialising in human rights law and, in particular, the rights of the child. He has extensive casework and research experience and is a visiting lecturer at Queen Mary and Westfield College, University of London. He is a research associate at the Programme on the International Rights of the Child and is on the Howard League Youth Justice Working Group.

The Legal Action Group is a national, independent charity which promotes equal access to justice for all members of society who are socially, economically or otherwise disadvantaged. To this end, it seeks to improve law and practice, the administration of justice and legal services.

Human Rights Act Toolkit

SECOND EDITION

Jenny Watson and Mitchell Woolf

 Legal Action Group
2007

This edition published in Great Britain 2007
by LAG Education and Service Trust Limited
242 Pentonville Road, London N1 9UN
www.lag.org.uk

While every effort has been made to ensure that the details in this text are correct, readers must be aware that the law changes and that the accuracy of the material cannot be guaranteed and the author and the publisher accept no responsibility for any losses or damage sustained.

British Library Cataloguing in Publication Data
a CIP catalogue record for this book is available from the British Library.

ISBN 978 1 903307 61 8

Typeset and Printed by Hobbs the Printers, Totton, Hampshire.

Foreword to the first edition

by HELENA KENNEDY QC,
Doughty Street Chambers, London

The law is too important to be left to lawyers. Nowhere is this more true than in the field of human rights. On 2 October 2000 I and many of my colleagues celebrated what was a truly historic occasion – the coming into effect of the Human Rights Act 1998. This was not – as the tabloids would have had us believe – because the Act represented some sort of gravy train for over-paid lawyers; it was rather because it marked a significant milestone on the road towards what many, including organisations like LAG, Liberty, Justice and Charter88 had long campaigned for – 'a popular culture of rights'.

However the Human Rights Act was a milestone, not a destination. In order to achieve a genuine shift in our democratic culture, human rights thinking needs to be moved out of academia, the courts and oak-panelled rooms in barristers' chambers and into the workplace and the public sphere.

The core values that the Human Rights Act seeks to promote are those of mutual respect and the dignity of the individual. That the Act redefines the relationship between the individual and the state and its agencies should not be viewed as some new, complex and foreign form of the much-reviled political correctness – a maze of obscure rules lying in wait to trap the unwary. Rather it should be seen as a positive expression of a mature society.

Section 6 of the Human Rights Act begins 'It is unlawful for a public authority to act in a way that is incompatible with a Convention right'. There is mounting evidence that, within many public bodies, awareness of the Act has not progressed beyond the legal department. It has not filtered through to the people who really matter – those at the sharp end of providing public services. A genuine human rights culture – one in which respect and dignity are paramount – will emerge not as a direct result of legislation, but when hard-pressed public sector workers are engaged with the issues, and empowered to make decisions about their everyday work.

These are the people who will ultimately determine the success or failure of the Act.

In this context I warmly welcome this wonderfully useful book. The checklists are gems of straightforward practicality – matched only by the beautifully succinct and clear explanation of human rights principles. I sincerely hope that this book is the success it deserves to be. When well-thumbed copies can be found on the desks of busy managers in public authorities across the land, I will know that the heady optimism of that day in October 2000 was justified.

Helena Kennedy QC
Member of the House of Lords

February 2003

Contents

Introduction

Introduction

1.1   *Human Rights Act Toolkit* is an introduction to the Human Rights Act 1998. The *Toolkit* is a guide to the law, but it is primarily designed for managers: it assumes the reader has no knowledge of the Act already. Lawyers who have not specialised in human rights law may also find the *Human Rights Act Toolkit* useful. The *Toolkit* can be used to find out more about the Act, as a checklist to audit new or existing policies and procedures or to help when considering the Human Rights Act in a decision making process.

Why do I need to know about the Human Rights Act?

1.2   The Human Rights Act 1998 is a law which came into force in the UK in October 2000. It gives new rights to individuals to challenge decisions made by public bodies. The Act applies to all public bodies – for example local authorities, government departments and the National Health Service – as well as to some charities and private companies if they provide public services under contract. Since October 2000 it has been against the law for staff working in these organisations to breach people's human rights. The Human Rights Act is a minimum standard that everyone has to reach and that no one should fall below.

1.3   During the debates in Parliament as the Act was becoming law, the government was explicit in its vision of the outcome that it would produce. They hoped the Human Rights Act would help to develop 'a human rights culture' in the UK: one where all of us would be treated with the dignity and respect that all human beings deserve. Already it has had a tremendous impact, shown by the case-law that has developed as judges have been asked to apply the Act in a wide range of court cases. But it has not yet led to human rights practice becoming common within public bodies. Sadly it has also led to many media myths about the Act. Most of these are not true.[1] Of those that are, many are caused by a misunderstanding of the Act, or are due to poor legal advice. In some cases the human rights of one

---

1   For a review of these myths see the DCA's *Review of the implementation of the Human Rights Act,* July 2006, at www.justice.gov.uk

individual have not been balanced against the rights and interests of others, or of the wider community. Using this *Toolkit* to increase your understanding of the Act should ensure that staff in your organisation are less likely to make such basic errors of judgment and that they can confidently balance rights against each other.

1.4   Everyone working in a public body – and in those charities and private companies that could be covered by the Act – should be aware of the impact of the Human Rights Act. If you or your colleagues make decisions about service delivery or about new policies and procedures that could impact on people's human rights, you need to be able to demonstrate that human rights have been taken into account before the decision is made. Managers and staff in public bodies need good guidance to enable them to make sense of the Act, and see how to use it in their day-to-day work. This *Toolkit* is designed to provide just that.

1.5   But perhaps more importantly than this compliance framework, the Human Rights Act also provides a useful management tool to help you think through complex judgments in your everyday working life. For example people working in such varied areas as a social worker trying to decide what action to take to protect a child at risk, a probation officer dealing with an offender on bail, an environmental health officer faced with protests from local residents about late night noise and violence caused by users of a local nightclub or a police officer trying to decide how to protect a woman experiencing domestic violence could all apply a human rights framework to ensure that they carefully balance the competing interests in their situation: the framework can help to ensure that nothing is missed and that the decision making process is objective. Of course, no judge will expect staff in public services, charities or private companies to make decisions as if they have studied the law for many years. But the point of this framework is not to turn us all into lawyers: it is to give us a better tool to use when making some of the difficult and competing judgment calls that those who run our public services make every day.

What kind of rights are human rights?

1.6   The Human Rights Act brings a wide range of rights under the protection of UK law. It guarantees everyone living in the UK – whether or not they are a UK citizen – the following rights:

- the right to life;
- the right to be free from torture, inhuman or degrading treatment;
- the right to be free from slavery;
- the right to liberty;
- the right to a fair trial or fair hearing;
- the right to respect for your private and family life and your home;
- the right to respect for freedom of thought, conscience and religion;
- the right to free expression;
- the right to freedom of association and assembly;
- the right to marry and have a family;
- the right to peaceful enjoyment of your own possessions and property;
- the right to an education;
- the right to free elections; and
- the right not to be discriminated against in the enjoyment of any of these rights.

1.7   These rights originate in an international human rights treaty, the European Convention on Human Rights. Much of this treaty has now become part of UK law through the Human Rights Act. This treaty was drawn up after the Second World War, when the scale of human rights violations in Europe horrified the world. In Nazi Germany the human rights of Jews, Gypsies, Slavic people, opposition political activists, trade unionists, lesbians and gay men, people with learning difficulties and disabled people were routinely abused and violated, leading many to either labour camps or extermination camps. The Universal Declaration of Human Rights, signed by the General Assembly of the United Nations in 1948 was intended to send a signal that this should never happen again. The ECHR, signed by countries that joined the Council of Europe, was an attempt to do the same on a regional level. The UK was the first signatory to the ECHR in 1950. More information about these human rights, what they mean in everyday language and how some of them can be restricted in certain circumstances, is provided in chapter 2 and in more detail in chapter 8.

What happens if we get it wrong?

1.8   If your organisation fails to adequately protect people's human rights, or fails to take account of the Human Rights Act in its decision making, it can be taken to the UK courts – and might be forced to pay damages. It isn't possible to defend your organisation by arguing that a member of staff breached an accepted policy: that their actions were a one-off. It's still the organisation that will be on trial. Defending a challenge in court is expensive, time-consuming, and of course it can also involve risks to reputation. If your organisation is found to have breached human rights, it could be left with a bad name, and be put under more scrutiny by audit bodies.

1.9   Despite this, research carried out by the then District Audit in 2002[2] suggested that 56 per cent of the public bodies they surveyed had no clear corporate approach to ensure that their policies were compliant with the Human Rights Act. In health bodies this figure was even higher – 65 per cent. Almost half of all public bodies had failed to give their front-line staff any support that could help them to understand the Act and almost 80 per cent of respondents had taken no action at all to ensure that contractors or subsidiary bodies complied with the Act. Many said they simply left their legal department to deal with the Act and its implications. This is not a strategy that can effectively prevent legal challenges in court. Of course, from time to time, legal advice will be needed in relation to a particularly tricky issue but human rights principles are principles that everyone can use and understand. Applying these principles in everyday situations can help to avoid legal challenge. That is the purpose of the *Human Rights Act Toolkit*.

I don't work for a public body: do I still need to know?

1.10   The Act has the potential to reach out much more widely than just to public bodies. For example, charities that provide services under contract to local government or private companies that want to win government tenders also need to understand the Act. Increasingly, contracting bodies are starting to specify in their tender documents that any contracts awarded must be provided in line with the Human

---

2   *The Human Rights Act, a bulletin for public bodies*, District Audit, 2002.

Rights Act. Sometimes clients or service users who want to ensure that their human rights are respected will ask to have this specified in private contracts, for example older people who want to find residential care. So you may need to understand the Human Rights Act even if you don't work directly for the government.[3]

I'm not a lawyer: will I understand it?

1.11   *Human Rights Act Toolkit* is designed for people who have no legal knowledge and is based on the application of human rights principles to everyday work. There is no need to understand the detail of the law to be able to use the Human Rights Act as a decision making framework. If you can identify the values and principles that are contained within the Act, and apply these, you will be well on the way to delivering the human rights culture that the government hoped the Act would generate and of course the organisation that you work for will be much better protected against any legal challenge in the courts. If you want more detail about the law itself, you will find it in the second section of the *Human Rights Act Toolkit*.

1.12   In any case many of the principles that underlie the Human Rights Act will be familiar from existing good practice. Making them explicit in a work context can mean that your organisation avoids conflict and is better able to demonstrate that the individual – the service user or the client – is always at the centre of the decision making process. The Human Rights Act framework of 'balancing rights' can also help you to ensure that your decisions are objective and can be justified. It is this framework which helps to give the Act its relevance as a management tool.

The Human Rights Act as a management tool

1.13   The Human Rights Act is concerned with ensuring that the rights of the individual are balanced against the rights of others and the interests of the community. By using this human rights framework to help with decision making, services can deliver the best outcome for everyone concerned. Treat the Human Rights Act as a management tool: its principles can help deliver the best possible

---

3   You can find out more about this in chapter 11.

standards of service that resources will allow by ensuring that the individual remains at the heart of the service. The Act can also help in understanding where resources may need to be targeted in the future by helping to identify groups or individuals whose perspectives might not previously have been considered. Using the Act in this way will help you to avoid some of the poor decision making that has been blamed on the Act during the past few years. It makes it explicit that the rights of the individual must be balanced against other competing rights and interests – whether of other individuals in the situation or of the community as a whole – and that this balancing act means that people's rights can, of course, be restricted when these restrictions are justified. For example it does not breach anyone's human rights to require a driver caught speeding on camera to tell the police who was driving the car at the time: indeed that might help the state to protect the right to life, particularly of children, by ensuring that safe speed limits operate in residential areas.

1.14   So, using a human rights framework can help you make better decisions, demonstrate to service users that the decision making process is objective, and protect your organisation against allegations that it has not considered people's rights. The framework can also be a source of good practice even where internal procedures do not – in strict legal terms – need to be compliant with the Act. If you use the Act in this way, it is far from being the burden that some commentators suggested prior to its introduction. It may even help you develop and provide the type of individualised public services that people have increasingly come to expect. It will certainly help you to manage risk and to avoid poor service outcomes.

How does the *Human Rights Act Toolkit* work?

1.15   *Human Rights Act Toolkit* introduces basic human rights principles. These are easy for everyone to understand: they don't demand any legal knowledge. The question and answer format of the checklist, and the examples throughout the book, will help explain how these principles are applied in real life situations. There is a clear but more detailed explanation of the Act in the second section of the *Toolkit*.

Part I: The checklist

1.16   The first part of the book is a step-by-step question and answer format – a checklist. This is designed to help to make the principles relevant to your own responsibilities, and prompt you to apply them to the decisions that you have to make on an everyday basis. Chapter 2 covers the Act as a whole, followed by separate chapters that cover two particularly important areas of the Act – a mini-checklist to the decision making process, and a mini-checklist on discrimination. All of the checklists have case study illustrations, and examples of situations in which the Human Rights Act and the principles behind it could apply. Worked case study examples are included at the end of this section to illustrate the whole process. The checklist process is shown as a diagram on page 20. You can use the checklist to help you gain a better understanding of the Act, or you can use it as a tool to audit policies and procedures.

Part II: The law

1.17   The second part of the book gives a much more detailed explanation of the Human Rights Act in non-legal language. Lawyers who have not specialised in human rights may find this part of the *Toolkit* particularly helpful. Chapter 7 explains the development of human rights thinking in Europe and the UK to provide some context. This is followed by chapters explaining in detail all the rights protected by the Human Rights Act, and a more detailed description of the types of rights and obligations that are now imposed under the Act. Chapter 10 explains human rights principles in detail, and shows how judges have been guided by them when applying both the Act and the European Convention on Human Rights. The final chapter in this section explains how the Human Rights Act itself works, and how it interacts with the legal system in the UK.

1.18   In Part III you will find the full text of the Human Rights Act 1998.

How do I use the *Toolkit*?

1.19   Reading the Human Rights Act Toolkit through from start to finish is the fastest way to learn more about the Human Rights Act. But the checklists are designed primarily to be used to sort out practical problems and there is more information to help you do so in the next chapter. They can help audit existing policies, assessing assumptions against the new human rights principles. Also they can be used to help draft new policies and procedures or to help you make decisions. They can be used alongside existing standards or pieces of legislation or guidance. The checklist can also be used to help inform a service review or other inspection.

1.20 The checklist acts as a prompt to consider human rights principles. As the Human Rights Act is a new decision making framework, in some cases, it will challenge you to think differently but it also gives your organisation confidence that human rights have been considered as part of the decision making process.

PART I

The Checklist

CHAPTER 2

The Human Rights Act checklist

2.1	**Introduction**
2.4	**Why do we need this checklist?**
2.9	**How to use this checklist**
2.12	**The checklist process**
2.13	Section one – the policy area or decision making process
2.14	Section two – identification of rights
2.15	Section three – protection of rights
2.16	Section four – balancing rights
2.17	Section five – organisational process
2.18	**Mini checklists**
2.19	The right to a fair trial
2.20	Discrimination
2.21	**Section one – the policy area or decision making process**
	1.1 What is the decision, policy or process that is being developed?
	1.2 Why is it needed and what is its purpose?
2.24	**Section two – identification of rights**
2.25	**Rights protected by the Human Rights Act**
	Article 2 • Article 3 • Article 4 • Article 5 • Article 6 • Article 7 • Article 8 • Article 9 • Article 10 • Article 11 • Article 12 • Article 14 • Article 1 of protocol 1 • Article 2 of protocol 1 • Article 3 of protocol 1

2.1   Make a note of any rights that could be affected, and identify whose rights they are

2.2   Look again at each of the rights identified in 2.1. Will the decision, policy or process impact on any of these rights, and if so is it to protect them or interfere with them in a way that might restrict them? Give an answer for each right identified

2.48   **Section three – protection of rights**

3.1   The Human Rights Act may impose a positive obligation (or special duty) to protect some rights. Is there any way in which this could be relevant?

3.2   If you have answered 'yes' to question 3.1, identify whose rights are affected

3.3   Identify the action that might need to be taken to protect these rights

3.4   Who needs to know about this action and who has the final responsibility to make sure that it happens?

2.63   **Section four – balancing rights**

4.1   Think about the person whose rights are restricted. How will they find out about the impact of the decision your organisation wants to make?

4.2   Identify the legitimate aim that you are trying to meet

4.3   Are you restricting one person's rights to protect the rights of another individual? If so, explain whose right will be restricted, whose protected, and why is this necessary

4.4   Is there another way to achieve the aim identified in question 4.2? If there is note it

4.5   What is the reason for not adopting the approach identified in the answer to question 4.4?

4.6   Think about the diversity of clients, staff and service users that your organisation works with. Would the answer to question 2.2 be different if considered from another perspective? If so, how?

2.84 **Section five – organisational process**

5.1 Who has been consulted about this policy or procedure?

5.2 Who must agree to the policy or procedure before it can be finalised?

5.3 How will people get the training and information they need to ensure that the policy or procedure works?

Introduction

2.1   This checklist will explain the new framework that the Human Rights Act provides and show how it will impact on your area of work. It enables you to consider the rights protected by the Act through a series of simple questions, and to assess whether the policy or procedure your organisation wants to develop might impact on these rights. It is designed for non-lawyers: managers, policy specialists or for other staff needing to understand the Act, but who approach it from a non-legal perspective.

2.2   This is the main checklist. It is followed by two mini checklists which cover people's European Convention on Human Rights (ECHR) article 6 rights to a fair trial or hearing, and their article 14 rights to be free from discrimination.

2.3   More detailed information about the Act is set out in the Part II of the *Human Rights Act Toolkit*.

Why do we need this checklist?

2.4   The Human Rights Act makes it unlawful for any public authority (which can include a charity or private company in some circumstances) to act in a way that contravenes rights protected by the European Convention on Human Rights. Violations of human rights can now be challenged in British courts. You can read more about this in greater detail in Part II of the *Human Rights Act Toolkit*.

2.5   In many cases, your organisation's existing good practice will meet the high standards set by the Human Rights Act. In some cases – because the Act brings new concepts and new responsibilities into British law – it may not. So this checklist is a helpful framework to consider how the Act is relevant to your work. You can use it to help you understand the Human Rights Act as a set of principles. Or you may want to use it to see if any changes to policy or procedures may be necessary to remain compliant with the HRA. You are not expected to act like a lawyer, but public service providers, and to a lesser extent head teachers and governing bodies are increasingly expected to understand a human rights framework. This checklist is designed to help you understand the principles that lie behind the Act, and do just that.

2.6   The checklist is designed to give an opportunity to assess whether your policy will comply with the Human Rights Act, or to prompt you to seek legal advice should it be needed. It is not a legal document. It can be filled in using the same kind of language that you would use to make notes on any work related issue.

2.7   Importantly for your organisation, if you use it to audit policies the checklist may also provide an opportunity to demonstrate, in the case of a legal challenge under the Act, that Human Rights Act issues were considered when the policy or process in question was drafted, or that decisions were made within the new framework of the Act. It gives an opportunity to show that the policy or procedure was considered from the perspective of a wide range of users, and that attempts were made to ensure that it balanced different people's rights and could be applied flexibly if necessary.

2.8   The courts have called the Human Rights Act a 'living instrument'. They expect the rights that are protected by the Act to be applied in the light of changing social conditions. The checklist can also help to review policies, to ensure whether they are in line with modern interpretations of human rights.

How to use the checklist

2.9   The checklist is designed to provide an opportunity to use a Human Rights Act framework in day to day decision making. This checklist is a good introduction to the Human Rights Act as a management tool. When a new policy is being designed, it is useful as a prompt for a team discussion. It can be used as a backstop against which to check existing policies or thinking, and it can be used as a reference book to remind you of the principles and framework that lie behind the law. Alternatively you might use the checklist as an easy to read explanation of the law itself. However you use it, working through the questions on the checklist will take a little while at first, but will become second nature over time. You can miss sections if you want, and it may be clear if a section is not relevant, but bear in mind that the checklist is a structured process. It is designed to cover a number of important human rights principles, and you may miss one that is important if you skip from section to section.

2.10   After most of the questions there are guidance notes and case illustrations. The guidance notes explain each question. They act as a step-by-step guide to the process of completing the checklist. The case illustrations give examples from real cases or issues that have arisen during the work of public bodies to demonstrate how the Act applies in practice. They illustrate the broad principles behind the Act, showing how they impact on different situations and cover a wide range of areas, from social services to planning and licensing. Together, these should answer any questions about the Act. Reading the guidance notes straight through from beginning to end will give a clearer understanding of the checklist process before you start to use it, as well as giving you a better understanding of the rights protected by the Human Rights Act.

2.11 The worked case studies at the end of this section show the checklist in use in more detail. It can be used to audit a policy or procedure that has already been drafted, or it can be used to help develop a new policy on a step by step basis. Either way, it uses the Human Rights Act framework to ensure that the Act has been taken into account. When the checklist has been completed, there may be more action to be taken – for example talking with a colleague, referring an issue to a manager, or taking legal advice. If there is no action to be taken and the policy is implemented, the notes taken as the checklist is worked through could be useful in the future if a legal challenge is brought. They will demonstrate that the Act has been considered in the decision making process.

The checklist process

2.12 The main checklist itself has five sections covering different areas of the Human Rights Act. They are set out below. Working through each section in turn enables you to be sure that you have covered the Human Rights Act from different perspectives, and to have confidence that you have considered people's human rights adequately before a final decision is made.

Section one – the policy area or decision making process

2.13 This provides the context for the decision or policy audit, and sets out the context within which a Human Rights Act framework will be applied.

Section two – identification of rights

2.14 This identifies the human rights on which a policy or decision might impact, and starts to explore the important concept of balancing rights, where different people's human rights may be weighed against each other. If the right to a fair trial (article 6) or the non-discrimination clause (article 14) are identified as relevant at this stage, the checklist prompts you to complete the relevant mini checklist.

Section three – protection of rights

2.15   This section covers the important duty that your organisation may now have to protect people's rights. In some cases, the organisation that you work for may even have a duty to protect one individual from the actions of another, even if this action is out of your direct control. This duty is called a positive obligation. It is an important new concept imposed by the Human Rights Act. This section will also identify action that needs to be taken to meet this obligation.

Section four – balancing rights

2.16   This section explores further the concept of balancing rights, enabling you to identify whether the action you intend to take to restrict a person's rights is justified and proportionate. The concept of proportionality is another important part of a Human Rights Act framework.

Section five – organisational process

2.17   The final section of the main checklist identifies the necessary internal steps that need to be taken to ensure that your organisation can be confident that staff and contractors are able to apply the policy in line with a Human Rights Act framework.

Mini checklists

2.18   The main checklist is followed by two mini checklists each covering an important area of the Human Rights Act.

The right to a fair trial

2.19   The first mini checklist enables you to assess the impact of article 6 – the right to a fair trial or hearing – on your work, identifying the principles which shape a fair hearing. It also enables these principles to be applied to the creation of a consultation process.

Flowchart of steps in Human Rights Act checklist

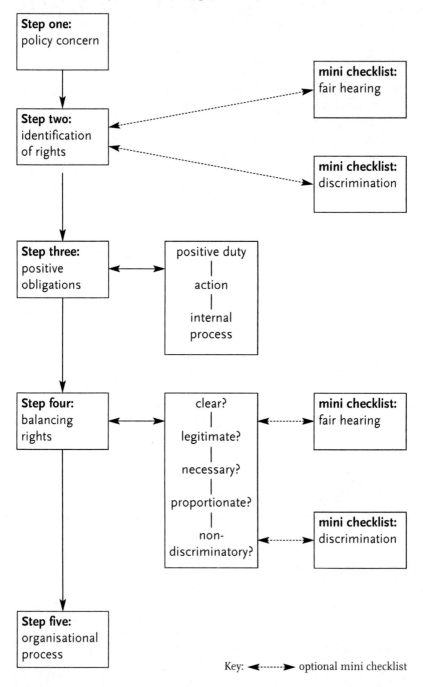

Discrimination

2.20 The second mini checklist ensures that you understand the full impact of article 14, the non-discrimination clause protected by the Human Rights Act, and are able to assess its impact on your work.

You can see the full process set out as a diagram.

Section one – the policy area or decision making process

1.1 What is the decision, policy or process that is being developed?

1.2 Why is it needed and what is its purpose?

2.21 These questions cover the basics – why is the policy being developed, why is it needed, and what is its purpose?

2.22 This section ensures that all the information about the new policy is together in one place should someone else in the organisation need to know about it, perhaps to provide additional help or advice. If you need to seek legal advice, it will provide a legal department or external solicitor with the context that they need to understand what the policy is for and why it is needed. It is also useful information to keep for the future. Staff turnover might mean that if a legal challenge is brought, the reasons for the policy have to be pieced together by people who were not involved at the time. These notes can help to avoid this.

Case illustration: reasons for development of a new policy

An NHS funded drop-in centre run by a charity provides help and services for people who have mental health problems and alcohol dependency. There is a risk assessment process in place, and every client is assessed before they can use the service. Clients' behaviour inside the centre is considered to be part of the assessment.

Staff are becoming increasingly concerned that one service user is unpredictable, often racist and on occasions has had

---

episodes of violent behaviour in the local area around the centre. Recently he assaulted another client just up the road from the front entrance, and he frequently shouts racist abuse at passers by. The staff believe that the risk assessment process must change to incorporate this type of incident, even though this may mean denying a client access to the service, or providing the service in a different way. They want to protect staff from potential risk, but also to protect the rights of the general public, and of other service users. They hope to use a Human Rights Act framework to amend the risk assessment process in an appropriate way.

2.23   Question 1 is particularly important. It enables the reasons why the policy is needed to be set out. If something has happened to prompt your team or department to draw up a new policy, it should be included here. This might include the need to react to one-off or high profile incidents that mean your organisation needs to act if it is to protect people's human rights from the actions of others, or may need to limit an individual's rights in the public interest. It may be prompted by a review of existing risk assessment procedures, or it could be a reaction to new government legislation or regulations, or guidance from another regulator. The answer to this question can be quite general since it will be covered in more detail later in the checklist.

Section two – identification of rights

2.24   This section of the checklist explains the rights protected by the Human Rights Act and enables policies and procedures to be considered for their impact on these rights. More detailed information about these rights – known as Convention rights – can be found in Part II of the *Human Rights Act Toolkit* and the text of the Act itself is set out in Part III. There is more information on the internet and the Ministry of Justice publishes other useful summary booklets on the Act.[1]

---

1   www.justice.gov.uk, and www.direct.gov.uk/en/RightsandResponsibilities/ citizensandgovernment/DG_4002951.

Rights protected by the Human Rights Act

Article 2

2.25 The *right to life* gives the right to have your life protected by law. Everyone in the UK has this right – even people who have committed serious criminal offences.

Article 3

2.26 Gives you the absolute *right not to be tortured or subjected to treatment or punishment that is inhuman or degrading.* Inhuman treatment can include serious physical assault. Degrading treatment can include ill-treatment that is grossly humiliating: bullying or institutional racism might reach this threshold. Remember that degrading treatment does not have to be intentionally degrading. Its impact is what is important. Part II of the *Human Rights Act Toolkit* explains this in more detail.

Article 4

2.27 Gives you the *right not to be subject to slavery or forced labour.* This does not mean that you have the right to be paid for everything you do – for example unpaid work as part of a community service order, or in a prison would not breach this right.

Article 5

2.28 Gives you the *right to liberty and security of person.* It means that you should not have your liberty taken away from you through arrest or detention except in the circumstances set out in the article itself.

Article 6

2.29 Gives you the *right to a fair trial.* It applies to both civil and criminal matters. It can also apply to dismissal from employment, to the withdrawal of benefit, or to a decision to withdraw a license to practice a profession. The right to a fair trial may be relevant to the disclosure of evidence to two sides in a case, or to the procedures adopted for certain kinds of hearings. A separate mini checklist at chapter 3 will explore this right in more detail.

Article 7

2.30   Gives you the *right not to receive punishment without law*. If you do something that was not against the law, or other regulations, at the time, you cannot be penalised for it later.

Articles 8-11 can all be restricted in the interests of others. Section four of the checklist will deal with this in more detail.

Article 8

2.31   You have the *right to respect for your private and family life, your home and correspondence*. This gives us a right to privacy in British law for the first time. It also includes what the courts call 'bodily integrity' – no one can interfere with your body unless you consent to it (for example in the case of an operation). The principle of autonomy – being in control of the decisions that we all make through life – is also important, particularly for disabled people or older people, including for those who use public services. Domestic violence or sexual abuse could be a breach of article 8 rights, as could restrictions placed on friendships or relationships between older people or disabled people living in residential care. A fair decision making procedure is particularly important in relation to article 8 rights. If you identify this right as one affected by the policy or decision that is being considered, the mini checklist in Chapter 3 below which deals with article 6 rights will also be relevant.

Article 9

2.32   You have the *right to respect for freedom of thought, conscience and religion*, which extends to the ability to practise or show your religious or other deeply held beliefs in public or in private.

Article 10

2.33   You have the *right to free expression*. You can say and write what you like and exchange information freely with other people – as long as it doesn't harm anyone else. For example, people who use the internet to exchange child pornography could not claim that they have the right to do so under the Human Rights Act.

Article 11

2.34 You have the *right to free assembly and association* in a peaceful way. You can also join a trade union. So this right might give service users the right to protest at funding cuts outside a council meeting for example.

Article 12

2.35 Men and women have the *right to marry and have a family*, in line with national law.

Article 14

2.36 You have the *right to enjoy all your Convention rights without discrimination*. This is the *non-discrimination clause*. It uses the idea of differential treatment: whether someone has been treated differently to another person in the same or a similar situation when they should not have been. But it also contains another important concept, making it clear that sometimes it can be right to treat people differently where there is existing inequality in order to compensate for this. Difference can be due to 'sex, race, colour, language, religion, political or other opinion, national or social origin, association with a national minority, property, birth or other status'. Article 14 can only be used if it is linked to another right – it is not free-standing. A mini checklist in chapter 4 deals with this in more detail.

Article 1 of protocol 1

2.37 Protects the *right to peaceful enjoyment of possessions*. People cannot take away things that are yours, except in limited circumstances – such as in the public interest for example when gun ownership is restricted. Even in cases like these, a law must be passed to enable property to be confiscated. This article does not prevent a country from having tax laws, though some people have tried to argue that it should. A fair decision making procedure is particularly important in relation to this area of rights. If the policy or process being developed could impact on article 1, protocol 1 rights, the mini checklist in Chapter 3 below which deals with article 6 rights will also be relevant.

Article 2 of protocol 1

2.38   Gives the *right to an education*. No-one can be denied access to the education system. This right makes it possible for parents to seek an education for their child which is *in line with the parents' religious and philosophical beliefs*.

Article 3 of protocol 1

2.39   Protects the *right to free elections* which must be free and fair, and take place using a secret ballot. But countries can still impose some qualifications on those who can vote: for example the voting age.

2.40   In addition, articles 1 and 2 of protocol 6 abolished the death penalty in peacetime.

2.41   The next box shows some examples of situations where the Human Rights Act might apply.

Case illustrations: everyday decisions that relate to the Human Rights Act

The Human Rights Act is closely linked with decisions made on a day to day basis by all kinds of public bodies, and other bodies providing services on behalf of the state. Here are just a few examples. More detailed illustrations of the impact of the Act are provided throughout the *Toolkit*.

- Decisions about the provision of life-saving treatment, involving judgments about quality of life – article 2
- Decisions about how best to safeguard vulnerable people, eg children in public care, from abuse – article 3
- Intervention when a child is on the 'at risk' register – article 3
- Decisions about whether or not to detain someone under the Mental Health Act, or whether to continue to detain them in a secure unit – article 5
- Decisions about whether or not to strike someone – such as a doctor, solicitor, or midwife – from their professional body's list of those approved to practise – article 6
- Decisions about a planning application – article 6
- Decisions about all kinds of welfare benefits – article 6
- Appeals to benefit review panels – article 6

- Decisions about adoption or fostering – article 8 (and article 6)
- Decisions about secret filming to catch illegal traders or people fraudulently claiming benefit – article 8
- Monitoring and review of care plans – article 8
- Decisions about evictions, tenancy hearings, or benefit hearings – article 8
- Decisions about housing allocation – article 8
- Decisions about continuing artificial nutrition and hydration for some patients – article 8
- Decisions about domiciliary care provision – article 8
- Decisions about travellers' sites – article 8
- Decisions about planning developments – article 8
- Decisions about the release of information that involves a negative effect on the environment – such as incinerator emissions – article 8
- Decisions about the type of clothing that someone can wear in the workplace – article 9
- Decisions about the provision of services as these relate to people's beliefs – article 9
- Decisions about politically restricted posts – article 10
- Decisions about preventing individuals from speaking to the media about service issues – article 10
- Decisions about withholding information from service users – article 10
- Decisions about allowing protests on public bodies' property – article 11
- Decisions about IVF treatment – article 12
- Decisions about access to services – and potentially all of the above – article 14
- Decisions about compulsory purchase of property to allow development – article 1, protocol 1 (and article 6)
- Decisions about the pruning and control of trees on private property – article 1, protocol 1
- Decisions about alcohol licences – article 1, protocol 1 (and article 6)
- Decisions about faith schools – article 2, protocol 1
- Decisions about choice of school, particularly involving religious belief – article 2, protocol 1

> - Decisions about school exclusions – article 2, protocol 1
>   (and articles 6 and 14)
> - Decisions about the way in which the electoral roll will be
>   kept – article 3, protocol 1

Having read the notes above, questions 2.1 and 2.2 will help you identify which rights may be relevant to your work.

2.1   Make a note of any rights that could be affected, and identify whose rights they are

2.42   This point requires you to identify any of the Convention rights protected by the Human Rights Act upon which the policy or procedure in question might have an impact. Remember that the Human Rights Act imposes a duty not to interfere with people's rights unless absolutely necessary. Sometimes a policy will raise a number of different human rights issues, involving different articles. That is common, and all the articles that could reasonably apply should be noted – as in the example overleaf.

2.43   To fulfil the requirements in **2.1** above think about the policy or procedure that is being developed and identify the rights that relate to it. When the rights have been identified, work out who could claim these rights. It might be that two people could claim the same right – perhaps the right to privacy. If this is the case it should be noted. A human rights framework will quite often generate this response and it is covered in more detail later in this section.

2.2   Look again at each of the rights identified in **2.1**. Will the decision, policy or process impact on any of these rights, and if so is it to protect them or interfere with them in a way that might restrict them? Give an answer for each right identified.

2.44   This question asks you to look at the rights you have identified in answer to the previous question, and to say how your policy will impact on them. Whether the policy will protect a right or interfere with it in a way that might restrict it, both should be noted here. Remember that the rights protected by articles 2, 3 and 4 are absolute. They cannot be restricted in any way, though public bodies may act to protect them of course. Some restrictions can be placed on the rights protected by articles 5, 6 and 12, and these are set out in the text of the articles themselves: they are very specific. Later sections of this checklist will cover in more detail the rights protected by articles 8, 9, 10 and 11 and article 1 of protocol 1 where more of a balancing act is necessary. Chapter 8 in Part II of the *Toolkit* has more detailed information on all these rights which may be helpful in some situations.

2.45   The answer to **2.1** will help in answering question **2.2**, because it identifies who might claim each right. That will help assess whether the impact of the policy is to interfere with, restrict, or protect people's rights. Sometimes one person's right may be restricted to protect another person's rights or those of the wider community. This is known as balancing rights, and section four will ask some more questions about this area. The case illustration that follows provides an example of balancing rights, where different people can rely on different rights in the same situation.

Case illustration: balancing rights

A local authority is asked to re-house an ex-offender and his family. His conviction was for child sex offences. The local authority needs to ensure that they are able to re-house the family in a way that both protects the offender's right to privacy, and his family's rights to their home, as well as ensuring that other children are not put at risk. They will therefore need to balance his article 8 rights with the rights of local children, specifically article 3 and article 8 rights.

So, the balance of rights looks like this:

- Local children – article 3 (an absolute right) and article 8 rights
- Ex-offender and his family – article 8 rights

The authority resolves this balance as follows:

- Safeguarding local children's rights is a priority.
- This can only happen through safeguarding the ex-offender's right to privacy. Without this he may be driven from his home, preventing the appropriate monitoring and reviews from taking place.

> - The offender's family will lose their original home but will be offered an alternative so their right to a home, though it is interfered with, is not significantly restricted.
> - The local authority, police and probation service have a positive obligation to protect the children's rights and will need to take steps to make sure that they do so.
> - If local parents try to use article 10, saying that they have a right to know where the man lives, the local authority can show that it has already balanced different rights against each other. It is putting the children's rights first by keeping his location out of the public domain.

2.46   If article 6 rights or article 14 rights have been identified in the answer to question **2.2**, the mini checklists in chapters 3 and 4 will also be relevant. The mini checklist on article 6 rights is also helpful if article 8 rights or article 1, protocol 1 rights will be affected by the policy or procedure. Procedural fairness – a fair decision making process – is particularly important when considering these rights.

> **Case illustration: procedural fairness**
>
> The local authority hears that the ex-offender and his family are unhappy with the decision that has been made, and want to appeal. The staff team wants to ensure that he has access to the same appeal process as anyone else and is not discriminated against because of his previous conviction (article 14). They want the appeal process to be based on article 6 principles as good practice, despite the fact that the appeal panel's decision can be challenged in court.

2.47   If the policy or procedure imposes an unintentional interference with or restriction on a right, the checklist will show this by now. Options might be to reconsider the policy or to think about ways in which the policy could be changed or amended to avoid interference with people's rights.

Section three – protection of rights

2.48   The Human Rights Act can in some situations impose a special duty – called a *positive obligation* – to protect rights. This can apply to a situation where one individual might cause harm to another – even if that harm is out of the control of your organisation. This part of the checklist enables you to make sure that this important responsibility has been thought through.

2.49   This duty is particularly relevant to article 2 and 3 rights because they are considered to be of such fundamental importance, as well as to article 8 rights which can impact on what the court describes as 'intimate interests' or physical integrity. More detail is provided about positive obligations in chapter 9.

2.50   For the purposes of the checklist the following principles are relevant. You have:

- a duty to provide a reasonable level of resources to individuals in order to protect a Convention right. This means that you may need to provide the necessary support to someone to help them protect their own rights;
- a duty to prevent breaches of Convention rights. This means that you may have to intervene to protect one individual from the actions of another – even if these actions are out of your direct control;
- a duty to provide information to those whose Convention rights are at risk. This means that you may have to provide more information than you would have done prior to the Human Rights Act, in order to allow individuals to make decisions to protect their own rights;
- a duty to respond to breaches of Convention rights. This means that if a person's rights are violated, you must do something in response, including investigating what has happened.

2.51   The state also has a duty to put in place a legal framework which provides effective protection for Convention rights. This duty is unlikely to be directly within the control of your organisation, however, and is not considered in detail as part of the checklist.

2.52   The following examples will help you to understand the concept of positive obligations. The first set of examples illustrates the application of the principles listed above. The second set of examples show everyday situations where public bodies may have a positive obligation to protect rights.

Case illustrations: positive obligations

Provision of resources to protect rights

A local authority in London took on responsibility for housing a family who had lost their home through mortgage arrears. The local authority eventually provided them with a house. The father was caring for his six children and his wife, who was a wheelchair user. The social services department assessed the mother's needs, and found that the property allocated by the council was unsuitable. Because of the stairs, the woman was confined to the lounge, and could not use the first floor accommodation at all. This caused particular difficulties because she was incontinent. The social services care plan recommended that the family be provided with specially adapted accommodation. One year later, the family had still heard nothing and were living in the same house. Their solicitor wrote to the local authority who failed to respond to the family's letters, or to an independent report of their needs. Eventually the family took the council to court. The court ruled that suitable accommodation should be provided within six months. It was not, and the family again brought the council to court. At this time, 20 months later, accommodation was finally offered. Throughout all this time, the council had not explained why it had delayed providing the accommodation, or told the family why it had not answered their letters. The court found that from the date of the care assessment the council had an obligation to take steps to enable the family to lead as normal a family life as possible. But they had not met this obligation which showed a lack of respect for private and family life; the family's article 8 rights. The council was ordered to pay £10,000 in damages.

Intervention to protect one person's rights from the actions of another person

A local authority social services team was taken to the European Court of Human Rights on behalf of four children who had been subjected to emotional neglect and abuse by their mother. This abuse went on over a period of four and a half years. It was only after that time that the local authority decided to seek an emergency protection order for the children, and to move forward with care proceedings. A child psychiatrist working on the case said that the children's experiences were 'horrific'. The court found that the local authority had failed in its positive duty under article 3 to protect the children from abuses of their rights. It had not intervened to protect the children from the actions of another individual.

A woman teacher was bullied and persecuted by pupils at her school because she was a lesbian. She took the school to court under the Sex Discrimination Act. She lost her case. However, the court said that if the bullying and persecution had taken place after the introduction of the Human Rights Act, there could have been a violation of her right to privacy (article 8). In that case, the school would have had to act to protect her rights from being violated by other individuals.

Provision of information to protect rights

A man was knocked off his bicycle by an unmarked police car. As he got to his feet, the car continued, knocked him down a second time, and broke his leg. He also suffered psychiatric damage. He complained to the police and the Police Complaints Authority (PCA) handled his case. He wanted to see what the investigation had produced, and be able to comment on any statements or findings. The PCA said that they could not release any information and that they did not believe they needed to do so to comply with article 3.

The judge did not agree. He said 'the claimant's legitimate interests cannot be adequately safeguarded without affording him an opportunity to comment upon factual statements made by those present at the scene at the time ... he does have a right to comment on the evidence of others.'

The judge said he believed that for the public to be confident that cases like these were properly investigated – and to ensure that there was no suspicion of collusion – in some cases, such as this, the victim did have the right to involvement. The provision of information helped to ensure that his article 3 rights were protected.

Responding to breaches of people's rights

A young man was held on remand in a cell shared with another prisoner. The young man was killed by his cell mate, who was suffering from severe mental illness. There was no inquest and because the prisoner responsible pleaded guilty to manslaughter due to diminished responsibility, there was no need for a full criminal hearing. The young man's parents felt that more should have been done to find out how their son died. They wanted to know why the authorities had not passed on the information that they held about the man who killed their son, since he was a serious risk to anyone with whom he shared a cell. Though there was an inquiry into his death it had no powers to make witnesses give evidence and two prison officers did not attend. The inquiry took place in private, and the young man's parents could not be legally represented or question witnesses. In fact they were only allowed to attend for three days of the proceedings. Because of this the court found that the inquiry did not meet the positive obligation under article 2 – the right to life – to hold an effective official investigation in response to a violation of someone's human rights.

Everyday situations where public bodies may have positive obligations to protect human rights

A head teacher hears reports that a child is being bullied but decides to wait for further direct evidence before acting on what she thinks is hearsay evidence. The child is beaten unconscious within the school grounds a couple of days after her decision. A potential failure to protect the child's article 3 rights – even article 2 if the child dies.

A child tells a staff member at a hostel for asylum-seekers that a man in the hostel has abused her. The staff member raises this with the child's family. The father does not want any action taken: he fears it will affect their asylum status if they are seen to 'complain'. Without police involvement, the other resident cannot be evicted. The staff member decides to respect the family's decision. A potential failure to protect the child's article 3 and 8 rights.

A local authority refuses to re-house a woman who has experienced domestic violence and fears her ex-partner may return to her home in future. They say they have no other properties, and that the police should take steps to protect her. A fortnight later her partner does return and she is taken to hospital with severe injuries. A potential failure to protect the woman's article 8 rights.

An organisation uses the Criminal Records Bureau to conduct checks on all members of staff who come into direct contact with the children who are their clients. A temporary administrative worker makes a mistake and 10 staff are not checked: there is no process in place to catch such errors. One of these staff subsequently abuses a child in the organisation's care. A potential failure to protect the child's article 3 and 8 rights.

A 14-year-old girl confides in a teacher at school that she fears she is to be taken on holiday over the summer break and forced to marry an older relative in her parents' country of origin. The teacher is newly qualified, the school has no protocol in place for such situations, and the child never returns to the UK. A potential failure to protect the child's article 3 and 8 rights.

Staff in a Benefits Agency office have expressed concerns about the unpredictable behaviour of one of their clients. He has made threats against members of staff. They want increased security to be in place when he comes for his next appointment. Their manager refuses, and applies the usual risk assessment process. On his next visit the client pulls a knife on a member of staff. A potential failure to protect the article 8 rights of staff – even article 2 rights if the staff member dies.

A local resident is told one morning that the council are about to cut down much of a lovely old walnut tree, growing in his back garden, because some of its branches overhang a public car park. The council are worried that if a branch falls, they could be sued. The man is angry that the council have not

> discussed this with him, and manages to persuade them to stop the work on that day. After some discussion, the council agrees that it only needs to take off one branch, which is proportionate to the risk that it faces. A potential failure to respect the right to property; article 1, protocol 1.
>
> A local council is asked for information about work on a building site, which was formerly a petrol station. Local residents believe the soil, which is being dumped close to their houses, may be contaminated. The council says that it is unable to release the information because of commercial confidentiality. A potential failure to protect the article 8 rights of residents if soil emissions damage their health.

3.1   The Human Rights Act may impose a positive obligation (or special duty) to protect some rights. Is there any way in which this could be relevant?

2.53   Reconsider articles 2, 3 and 8 in relation to your policy in the light of the positive obligations that may apply. The easiest way to do this is to apply the principles set out at the start of section three of the checklist, taking each right in turn. This checklist asks you to consider articles 2, 3 and 8 specifically because these are the areas most likely to be affected in day to day decision making, although they are not the only articles where positive obligations may apply – they also commonly arise in relation to articles 6, 10 and 11. More detailed information about positive obligations is provided in chapter 9. If your answer to this question is negative, you can move straight to section four of the checklist.

2.54   In addition, it is possible to apply a human rights framework in relation to risk management. This requires consideration of the most extreme situation that a public body can reasonably assume might arise. It might be that such a situation will never occur. However, if it is reasonable to assume that it might, it will need to be assessed against the Human Rights Act. It may only be then that the policy or procedure would impact on people's human rights – but it could have a substantial impact. Ask yourself what is the worst thing that could happen? If it did happen, would this policy be capable of providing a response to it? Would human rights be affected?

2.55 Remember that other people may use your policy to shape their responses to situations so this will need to be taken into account. Of course, there are limits on what can be predicted and there is no expectation that policies should be designed to respond to completely unforeseeable events. A lack of knowledge, or a lack of resources, might also have a justifiable impact on what can be provided. Look at what the European Court of Human Rights said in relation to the case of *Osman v UK*, where they defined when positive obligations arise, specifically in relation to article 2, the right to life. The court said that it must be established that:

> ... the authorities *knew or ought to have known at the time of a real and immediate risk* to the life of an identified individual or individuals from the criminal acts of a third party and that they failed to take measures *within the scope of their powers* which judged reasonably might have been expected to avoid that risk.

2.56 This principle has been applied more recently to a case involving child protection issues, where it is also relevant: this relates to article 3, the right to be free from torture, inhuman or degrading treatment.

2.57 This is an important and significant change. It means that public bodies may no longer be able to use the defence that they cannot be sued for negligence. In the future, if the issue relates to an abuse of human rights that is serious – relating to articles 2, 3 and possibly article 8 – the courts will apply this test. They will look to see if the authority knew or ought to have known that there was a serious risk, which the authority's actions, judged reasonably, could have prevented.

2.58 So it may not be enough to offer as an excuse 'we didn't know' if your organisation arguably should have made sure it had the information. Also it may not be enough to explain 'we didn't have the money or the staff' if the organisation's powers mean that it could be expected to act. The following scenarios show this principle applied in a work context.

Case illustrations: risk management and positive obligations

A member of staff in a care home is concerned about a client who hoards out of date food in her room. Some of the food could be dangerous if eaten – some of it is months, or even years past its sell-by date. The member of staff raises this issue with her manager. The manager replies that if the resident has bought the food with her own money, there is nothing that staff can do to take it from her because she has a right to privacy. The staff team think the manager is wrong. They think they may be failing to protect the client: her immune system is weak, and severe food poisoning could be fatal. As well as being negligent, they are failing to meet their positive obligations under article 8 if she becomes ill and article 2 if she dies: they have the knowledge, but are failing to act on it.

Zahid Mubarak was sent to Feltham, a Young Offenders' Institution, on a three month detention order for failing to follow a community order after he was convicted of a drug related offence. He was killed by his cell mate, Robert Stewart, who beat him to death with a table leg. His family wanted to find out what had happened, and why in particular a young Asian man had been placed in a cell with a known white racist, with a significant history of violence and a diagnosis of personality disorder. The government refused the family's demand for a public inquiry. But the family took a case to the House of Lords, relying on the Human Rights Act and the positive obligation under article 2 for an effective inquiry to be held into any death. They won their case. At the inquiry the head of the Prison Service at the time that the murder occurred said that the death was 'entirely preventable', and the inquiry report agreed that different operational practice, including risk management, could have meant that Zahid Mubarak would still be alive today. The Prison Service should have had a better awareness of the levels of racism in the prison, better methods for handling complaints about cell mates, and better procedures for dealing with young offenders with personality disorder, all of which could have safeguarded his article 2 rights.

The Osman family took a case to the European Court of Human Rights at Strasbourg. The case was long and complicated, but centred on the fact that a teacher at their son's school became obsessed with their child. The teacher harassed the child's friends, changed his name by deed poll to include the child's name, and finally when he lost his job threatened to 'do a Hungerford', referring to an incident in a

British town where a gunman shot and killed several people. The teacher did eventually shoot and kill the child's father, seriously wounding the child. The family said they did not believe that the police had done enough to protect them. When the case went to court the family's lawyers argued that the police had failed to meet their positive obligations in relation to a number of different areas, specifically article 2 rights. The court disagreed. They found that the police could not have known that the teacher had stolen a gun, and could not have known that his mental state had deteriorated so much that he was capable of such action. In order to realise this, the police would have had to make connections between some seemingly random and unconnected events. The family believed they should have received police protection. The courts said that there was no evidence in front of the police to demonstrate that this was necessary: they did not have the knowledge to make this decision, nor the resources to provide it without adequate evidence.

3.2 If you have answered 'yes' to question 3.1, identify whose rights are affected.

2.59 Think about the risk management scenario used to answer question 3.1. Identify whose rights are affected in this situation so that you can identify the kind of action that you would need to take to protect their rights. A 360 degree assessment process can be used, taking into account everyone in the situation, to ensure that the rights of as many groups of people as possible can be considered.

3.3 Identify the action that might need to be taken to protect these rights

2.60 The answer to this section will probably be a practical suggestion, or an idea for action that could protect the rights in question. It may involve inter-agency working to find the right answer. Remember that when dealing with articles 2 and 3, there is less ability to argue that resources are a constraint, because the rights protected by these articles are of such fundamental importance.

Case illustration: action taken by a public body to protect human rights

A housing association is asked to re-house a tenant who has experienced domestic violence. It has no other suitable properties for her and her children so cannot move her to a new address. However, it is concerned to protect her rights. The housing association asks the police, and Victim Support, to advise it on what else can be done. The eventual outcome is that an alarm is fitted to her flat, linked to the police station, and she is provided with a mobile phone that she can use to call the police at any time. In addition, the CCTV in the foyer of the block is upgraded. The housing association feels comfortable that it has done as much as it can to fulfil its positive obligations under the Human Rights Act, and make sure her article 8 rights (and potentially her article 2 rights) are protected.

3.4   Who needs to know about this action and who has the final responsibility to make sure that it happens?

2.61   This question will clarify who needs to know what action will be taken, and should make it very clear what everyone's part is in ensuring that it happens. It may involve discussions with other agencies or partner organisations to make sure that they are clear about why the policy is in place, and that they too understand what might be required. It may also involve making new frameworks or responsibilities very clear to contractors so that they are aware of their responsibilities. In some cases it might be helpful to involve the legal team at this point, to clarify any responsibilities that need to be defined in a contract.

2.62   In cases that involve positive obligations and relate to family issues, consultation with the person or people involved may be particularly important. The courts have placed a great deal of importance on procedural fairness in relation to family matters, and have made it clear that this means the person affected must be able to give their views.

Case illustrations: involving third parties in protecting rights

A head teacher is contacted by a caseworker from social services. The social services team have good reason to believe that a child is being abused, and have acted to take the child into public care while the case is investigated, protecting the child's article 3 and 8 rights. They need to alert the head teacher to ensure that the child's mother and aunt, who are both involved in the case, are not allowed to pick the child up after school until further notice. They give the school clear instructions, and contact details for the social work team if this happens, and tell the mother and aunt of their decision. The head teacher is responsible for ensuring that all other teachers know. Within the social work team, a lead officer has already been identified to work on the case.

An organisation with statutory powers that works with people considered to be vulnerable is having a new computer system installed. In the past, when new systems have been installed, there have been occasions where unauthorised staff accidentally gained access to confidential information. In one case, this meant that staff who had not been through a criminal records check were able to access names and addresses of child clients. The organisation wants to be sure that the contractor understands the implications of the positive obligations imposed by the Human Rights Act (HRA) to protect privacy. They insert a clause in the contract specifying that the contractor must comply with the HRA, and they talk through their understanding of article 8 rights with all those working on the project. They are comfortable that the contractor understands the level of responsibility that they must take - even though they are a private company – to ensure they meet the high standards set by the HRA.

Section four – balancing rights

2.63 This section considers the ways in which the policy or procedure may restrict someone's rights. As you already know from section two above, there are some rights that can be restricted under certain circumstances: these rights are called qualified rights. The previous section has explained that sometimes it is necessary to restrict one person's rights to ensure that another's are protected, particularly where positive obligations are imposed under the Human Rights Act. This *balancing of rights* is a crucial part of the human rights framework. One example of balancing rights has already been discussed in section two of the checklist. This section covers balancing rights in more detail.

2.64   Organisations cannot just go ahead and restrict rights without good cause. In order to make sure that people's rights aren't restricted unnecessarily, the Human Rights Act sets out a number of conditions that must be met for restrictions to be justified. Restrictions must:

- have a *clear legal basis* that people can know about and understand, so that they are able to see the consequences of their actions. A human rights framework does not allow for arbitrary decision making. All staff will need to be clear about policies and procedures and be able to work within them. Additionally, policies and procedures need to be clear to service users.
- Have a *legitimate aim*. The text of the articles below shows you the grounds that are allowed as legitimate if rights are to be restricted. Your policy or procedure must be designed to genuinely pursue the aims set out in the articles.
- Be *necessary*. Necessary does not mean the same as reasonable, or useful, or desirable. Necessary restrictions are based on good reasons, usually involving the protection of other people's rights. Your restriction must be necessary in a democratic society: you cannot simply stop people doing things you don't like.
- Be *proportionate* – go only as far as is necessary to achieve the objective. You can read more about this below.
- Not *discriminate* against a particular group or class of people. You can read more about this in the separate mini checklist on article 14 of the European Convention on Human Rights.

2.65   The concept of *proportionality* is an extremely important one, and lies at the heart of the human rights framework that you are applying by using the checklist. The following points need to be considered in order to assess whether or not the restriction that will be made could be regarded as proportionate.

- Are there reasons for the restriction?
- Is there a less restrictive alternative that could apply?

- Have you thought about the rights of those affected?
- Is there anything left of the right after your restriction is in place?

2.66   The checklist will work through each of these questions in turn. For now, read through the notes. The grounds for restriction are set out in the articles themselves and have been emphasised in the text below.

- Article 8 – you have the right to respect for your private and family life, your home and correspondence. This right includes what the courts call 'bodily integrity' which might impact on medical treatment, as well as the important principle of autonomy – a person's ability to have as much control as they can over their body and decisions about their lives.

  This concept of autonomy may be particularly important if you work with older people or with disabled people, who can struggle to secure the ability to make their own decisions. For example services on which they rely grow over time to be shaped around staff needs, such as domiciliary care where the latest evening visit is at six at night, which means older people can't choose when to go to bed. Or situations where the staff in residential care settings make decisions about meetings that young people can or can't attend; for example preventing young people with learning difficulties from attending local meetings of People First, an advocacy group run by and for people with learning difficulties.

  Article 8 also protects people's ability to form relationships with those they choose and to be allowed to develop their own personality. Restrictions can be placed on this right if they aim to address: *national security, public safety, the protection of the economy, the prevention of crime, the protection of health and morals, or the protection of the rights and freedoms of others.*

  The definition of 'home' is contested and caution may be necessary. Some court cases have found that a home does not have to be lawfully occupied; others have found that it does. The concept of 'home' does not depend on a country's law: rather it depends on the particular circumstances of the individual's situation, and whether there are sufficient links between the person and the property or land. Other court judgments have found that things like vandalism (if it is severe) and harassment can interfere with someone's right to peacefully enjoy their home, as can environmental issues such as pollution. The way in which you make decisions about people's article 8 rights can be as important as the final decision itself. Procedural fairness is particularly important and if your decision has an impact on article 8 rights you will need to read chapter 3 of the *Toolkit* as well.

Case illustration: article 8 and autonomy – artificial nutrition and hydration

Oliver Burke took a case to court to challenge the General Medical Council's guidelines on the withdrawal of artificial nutrition and hydration (ANH). He has spino-cerebellar ataxia, uses a wheelchair, and at some point in the future will be completely physically dependent on others for his care. In particular he will lose the ability to swallow. This means that if he is to continue to live, he will need ANH, or tube feeding. His mental capacity is not affected by his condition so he was able to make it very clear that he wanted to continue to receive ANH regardless of his pain and suffering. He did not want doctors to make a decision on his behalf to withdraw ANH from him as he did not want to die from starvation. The courts found that any doctor who withdrew ANH from Mr Burke, or another such patient, when this was contrary to the patient's wishes, would violate their article 2, 3 and 8 rights. In fact the judges were very plain: 'for a doctor deliberately to interrupt life-prolonging treatment in the face of a competent patient's expressed wish to be kept alive, with the intention thereby of terminating the patient's life, would leave the doctor with no answer to a charge of murder'. But the competence of the patient is important because the court also decided that there was no duty for a doctor to continue ANH if 'it was not considered to be in the best interests of an incompetent patient for him to be artificially kept alive'. The court found that the General Medical Council's guidelines were able to protect Mr Burke's rights in such a situation and they recommended that they should be widely promoted to doctors to ensure that disabled people could have confidence that they 'will be treated properly ... and that they will not be ignored or patronised because of their disability'.

Case illustrations: balancing article 8 rights

A family lived close to a waste treatment plant that polluted the local environment. A private company ran the plant, but the decision to allow planning permission had been given by the regional government. The family tried to get the government to close the plant, but the government refused, and fought them in the courts. Eventually, the European Court of Human Rights ruled that because the pollution was so bad, the government had failed in its duty to protect the family's article 8 rights. Its failure to act had made them suffer the pollution for a much longer period of time.

A family lived close to a chemical factory. Because of the nature of the products contained within the factory, it was considered by the government to be a 'high risk' company. There was information available to the authorities which clearly showed that there were dangers and risks to health present in the running of the factory. But the authorities didn't pass these on to the family immediately. Instead, they delayed for several years. The court found that this breached the family's article 8 rights. As the family did not have the right information, they could not make their own decisions and choices about whether or not living near to the factory was too dangerous.

A London man found that a water utilities company kept discharging surface water and water full of sewage into his front and back garden. His house was damaged and he asked the utilities company to pay him damages. The utilities company said that it was trying to provide a service for all and that it was not practical for them to stop this discharge from happening because it would cost too much. The courts disagreed. They said that the man's article 8 rights had been breached. The courts said that if an authority is acting in the interests of the community as a whole, it may have to pay compensation to individuals whose rights are infringed. This will make sure that a fair balance is struck between the interests of the individual and the interests of the community.

Two sisters with severe learning and physical disabilities lived with their mother and step-father in Sussex. They needed 24-hour care and assistance, including help with all activities of daily living. This meant that they needed to be lifted. At home, a hoist was often used to lift the young women to and from bed, or bath. But they enjoyed swimming, horse riding, and shopping, where no mechanical assistance was available. Even at home, sometimes they reacted badly to the hoist and would become distressed. The local authority said that it would not allow its staff to lift the young women manually under any circumstances: this was a blanket policy. As a result, the young women were not provided with care. They took a case to court. The court found that the young women's article 8 rights were affected by the council's blanket ban on manual lifting (and that their article 2 or 3 rights could be as well if, for example, they were left in their own excrement for any period of time or if they were left lying after a fall, particularly in a public place). It recognised that the care workers also had article 8 rights which needed to be protected and said that a balance needed to be struck. The judge said the young women's 'rights to participate in the life of the community and to have access to an appropriate range of recreational and cultural activities are so important that a significant amount of manual handling may be required'. So, some interference with the care workers' article 8 rights could be justified in the interests of the rights and freedoms of others, and by reference to a proportionate balance. Both the blanket 'no manual lifting' policy, and the failure of care workers to take the young women out of the house to shop, swim or go riding, or to restrict the time spent on these activities were unlawful.

A local authority in the north of England wanted to close two care homes for older people. It said there would be a full consultation with service users and their families. After a whole series of meetings, the council's Scrutiny and Review Panel met and decided to close the homes. The residents' solicitor challenged this decision in court using both article 6 and article 8 arguments. The judge found that there was no evidence to show that the council had considered the article 8 rights of the residents. Since these rights had not been considered, the council could not justify the interference with the residents' article 8 rights that would be caused by closing the homes. The judge ordered the council to reconsider the matter again and to consider the residents' article 8 rights before they made the decision to close the home.

- Article 9 – you have the right to respect for freedom of thought, conscience and religion, and must be able to practise or show your religious or deeply held beliefs in public or in private. This right to practice or manifest your religion or beliefs can be restricted if the aim of the restriction is *public safety, the protection of public order, health or morals, or the protection of the rights and freedoms of others.*

Case illustrations: balancing article 9 rights

A Quaker, with strong pacifist beliefs, brought a case against the UK government. He believed that it was wrong for the government to expect him to pay tax when some of the money would be spent on defence and arms. He wanted to be able to tell the government to spend that particular portion of his taxes on something else. The court did not agree. They felt that tax laws were general, applying to everyone in the country, and did not impact on his article 9 rights.

A religious group owned a building that they used as a place of worship. The building was on Green Belt land, usually set aside for conservation, where very strict planning laws apply. The group put in a planning application to change the use of the estate, to allow public religious worship. This was rejected. Opponents argued that their temple was spoiling the environment and causing a nuisance to local residents – and that this would increase if more people used the building. The group tried to overturn the ban. They felt that because there were so few places of worship available to them, the law should not apply to them in the normal way. The court disagreed. It found that article 9 rights do not normally justify breaking a law that everyone else would have to keep.

A woman complained to her local cemetery in Luton that her husband's ashes had been interred in a consecrated plot following his funeral. She was a humanist as was her husband and she had held a humanist funeral for him. The cemetery said that she could not move the ashes. She took a case to court. The judge agreed with her. The court found that her article 9 rights meant that she should be able to move her husband's ashes from a place where their burial was contrary to her humanist beliefs.

A young Muslim woman attended a mixed sex, mixed faith school, with a strict school uniform policy well promoted to parents and pupils alike. After two years at the school she decided that she wanted to wear the jilbab – a long coat, covering the whole body. Previously at school she, and her sister, had worn the shalwar kameez (a tunic and trousers), which was allowed under the school's uniform policy. The school asked her to leave and return when she was wearing uniform. The school tried repeatedly to persuade her to return, but her brother told teachers that he would not allow it unless she was properly dressed. The school felt confident that it was right. It had strong links with local Muslim communities, a Muslim head teacher and many Muslim governors, and had recently reviewed its uniform policy to update the dress code. Following this review it had introduced the ability for girls who wanted to do so to wear hijab (a headscarf). The young woman stayed away from school for two years and finally took legal action against the school. She argued that it had breached her right to respect for religious freedom. She lost her case. The courts decided that the school had not interfered with this right by requiring her to wear uniform, but that if they had, this would in any case have been justified in the interests of protecting the rights and freedoms of others since there were girls at the school who did not want to be pressured into wearing jilbab. The court found that article 9 did not require people to be able to manifest their religion at any time or place of their choosing. It also said that interference with this right would be harder to establish if a person had voluntarily accepted a role which did not enable them to manifest their belief when there were other means for them to do so. In this case there was a single sex school close by which allowed girls to wear the jilbab as part of school uniform which could have been an alternative. Parliament had given the school the ability to decide on uniform policy, and they had done so in a way which was proportionate, and that could be justified under article 9.

- Article 10 – you have the right to free expression – to give and receive ideas and information to and from others without interference. However, this right can be restricted if the aim of the restriction is *national security, public safety, the prevention of disorder or crime, the protection of health and morals, the protection of the rights and reputations of others.*

Case illustration: balancing article 10 rights

The BBC had video footage that was needed as part of the evidence in a case against two police officers. The BBC did not want to disclose the video. They said it was not usual for journalists to have to disclose information, or their sources. The courts disagreed. They said that in many cases it was right that journalists' information and their sources should be able to be kept secret but when there is a criminal trial in progress, giving evidence was a normal civic duty. After all, individuals would have to give evidence. So, it was right that these article 10 rights should be restricted in such a case.

• Article 11 – you have the right to free assembly and association in a peaceful way. You can also join a trade union. This right can be restricted if the aim of the restriction is national security or public safety, the prevention of disorder or crime, the protection of health or morals, or for the protection of the rights and reputations of others.

Case illustration: balancing article 11 rights

A group of young men used to gather in a shopping centre in Wellingborough. There were complaints about their behaviour, sometimes involving the police, and many people believed that they caused nuisance. Eventually the local council wrote to the young men, telling them that they were banned from the shopping centre. A lawyer for the youths took a case to court, saying that they had the right to gather wherever they chose. The court disagreed. It said that if they had been organising a demonstration or some other kind of peaceful assembly, they could have relied on their article 11 rights. But they could not expect to do so simply because they wanted to hang out in a shopping centre.

- Article 1, Protocol 1 – you have the right to peaceful enjoyment of your possessions. Public bodies cannot usually interfere with the things you own, or the way that you use these things. This does not stop the state enforcing a taxation system, or prevent compulsory purchase of property. Possessions can include shares, licences, fishing rights, leases, planning consents, and things like goodwill. People can be deprived of their possessions if it is *in the public interest and subject to the conditions provided for by law and by the general principles of international law.* In addition a state can enforce any laws it thinks are *necessary to control the use of property in the general interest or to secure the payment of taxes or other contributions or penalties.*

2.67   The test for restricting people's peaceful enjoyment of their possessions is slightly different than for the earlier rights covered in this section, though it still relies on the important principle of proportionality, and the questions that follow can be used to assess whether this is the case. People can be deprived of their possessions – have them taken away permanently – if the intervention is:

- lawful
- in the public interest;
- reasonably proportionate.

2.68   People can be deprived of control of their possessions – where there is an interference that is not permanent such as temporary seizure of assets like a car, or withdrawal of a licence – if this intervention is:

- lawful;
- in the public interest, or aimed at securing the payment of taxes or other contributions or penalties;
- deemed 'necessary' by the state.

Case illustrations: balancing article 1, protocol 1 rights

The Law Society suspected that four partners in a law firm were dishonest. They withdrew the partners' practice certificates pending a full hearing of their case. The partners objected and took the Law Society to court. They argued that the Law Society's action would cause irreparable harm to their company, and that it infringed their right to peacefully enjoy their possessions. The court disagreed. The judge said that the

---

Law Society had to consider the public interest in any case before it decided to take away the partners' certificates pending the hearing. If the Law Society suspected dishonesty it had to act to protect the public so its action was necessary. It was right to withdraw the practice certificates.

The Royal Parks Regulations prevent particular vehicles from driving through St James's Park in London. The police stopped a private hire car driver with seven passengers as he was driving through the park using these regulations. The driver challenged his conviction in court, saying it interfered with his right to peacefully enjoy and use his possessions where he chose to do so. The court disagreed. They found that restricting particular types of vehicle from particular areas did not involve an interference with the driver's human rights. The court said that stopping trade in an area of historic significance, or of natural beauty, was designed to preserve the area's character for the general public which was a legitimate aim – so even if the ban had interfered with the driver's human rights, it would have been proportionate.

2.69 Reading through the explanations and examples above will help you to answer the questions in this section. They will help identify whether the restrictions on people's rights caused by your decision meet the standards that the courts may expect under the Human Rights Act.

4.1 Think about the person whose rights are restricted. How will they find out about the impact of the decision your organisation wants to make?

2.70 Identify how the person – or group of people – whose rights are restricted will find out about the restriction. Thinking through this question will ensure that the restriction has a *clear legal basis*: that it is set out in law, in a rule or in guidance and is not arbitrary. How will people affected by it find out about it, and will they be clear when they have found out that their behaviour may have to change – or their rights be restricted?

2.71 If the policy or guidelines have existed for a long time and are being redrafted, or if breaching the policy could lead to severe sanctions such as eviction, the withdrawal of a service, the withdrawal of benefits, or the separation of a family it is particularly important to think about how people will find out about the change. The change of policy will need to be presented in a way that makes it clear to people, so that they can understand the consequences of their actions. This might mean making guidance or other rules publicly available, perhaps via the internet, other partner organisations, or through cross-agency working.

2.72   Procedural fairness is particularly important in relation to article 8 rights to respect for private and family life or your home, or to changes affecting property rights that might be protected by article 1 of protocol 1. The mini checklist in chapter 3 can help ensure that your decision making process meets Human Rights Act standards.

Case study example: clarity of information

A drug treatment centre provided by the NHS has a very strict policy that no drugs are allowed on the premises. Clients who are found with drugs are asked to leave. To make sure no drugs are delivered by post, every resident has their letters opened in front of them by a member of staff and can have their possessions searched. This rule is clearly explained to people when they sign up to use the service, and is clearly displayed on noticeboards around the centre. All the agencies that refer drug users to the centre are asked to explain the rule to people before making a referral. The centre believes that the interference with article 8 rights is necessary and proportionate. It is confident that since the use of drugs is against the law, and the centre's rule is so clearly displayed and explained, applying to every service user, it has complied with the need for restrictions to have a legal basis.

4.2   Identify the legitimate aim that you are trying to meet.

2.73   If a restriction on rights is identified in the earlier answer to question 2.2, you will need to identify here the legitimate aim that your organisation is trying to meet. Remember that a legitimate aim is one that meets one of the outcomes set out in the text of the articles themselves, such as the protection of public order, or national security.

2.74   If the aim that you want to achieve is not listed in the notes above, it is likely that the restriction will not be seen as legitimate, and legal advice may be necessary.

4.3 Are you restricting one person's rights to protect the rights of another individual? If so, explain whose right will be restricted, whose is protected, and why this is necessary.

2.75   This question asks you to identify whether one person's rights are to be restricted in order to protect another's – and if so why this is necessary. Earlier you read about balancing rights. Balancing different rights against each other is an essential part of a human rights framework, and often this balancing act helps to ensure that a vulnerable person's rights are respected. The balancing act may even help you to meet your positive obligations under the Human Rights Act. However, the balancing act must be fair – and necessary.

2.76   Remember that necessary does not mean the same thing as 'reasonable' or 'desirable', nor is something necessary simply because most people would agree with it. The checklist question should enable you to assess whether there is a real need for the restriction proposed. In most cases there will be. If there is, note it. The answer to question **1.2** may help you here if you are introducing the policy or procedure as a result of a previous incident.

Case illustrations: restricting rights – is it necessary?

The Housing Act 1996 allows housing providers to run an introductory tenancy system. This means that during the first 12 months of the tenancy, the local authority can seek a possession order from the courts to take back the property from the tenant. They do not have to prove why they want to do this, although they do have to go through a set process. Introductory tenancies are usually given to tenants who have been disruptive neighbours, or who have a history of rent arrears. Introductory tenancies have been challenged in the courts. The judges found that although they did interfere with tenants' article 8 rights, the interference was necessary, and responded to a pressing social need. The judges also thought that introductory tenancies were a proportionate response to that social need.

In another case the courts found that if tenants continue to breach a possession order because they are in rent arrears, an eviction order can be a proportionate response. In this particular case the council served the possession order but evicted the tenant five years later because possession proceedings took a long time to go through the courts. During this time the rent arrears had continued to rise. The courts felt that the possession proceedings were designed to meet a legitimate aim, even though they interfered with the tenant's article 8 rights.

A woman with learning disabilities did not want to move from a local authority residential setting to living in the community. She said that the local authority could not force her to move because she had the right to a home under the Human Rights Act (article 8). The courts found that there was an interference with her rights but the court also believed that the move would be of positive benefit, ensuring that the woman could live as a citizen in the community. The interference with her rights was therefore justified.

4.4   Is there another way to achieve the aim identified in question **4.2**? If there is, note it.

4.5   What is the reason for not adopting the approach identified in the answer to question **4.4**?

2.77   These questions relate to the important concept of *proportionality*. The easiest way to describe proportionality without using any legal language at all is to say that you don't take a sledgehammer to crack a nut. Everyone knows what that means!

2.78   The legal thinking behind the Human Rights Act explains it as having a rational connection between the aim and the policy that restricts a person's rights. This means that the policy must go only as far as it needs to in order to achieve the aim. In some cases the blanket application of a policy to everyone, regardless of their individual needs, might be considered to be disproportionate. The courts have said that they may pay attention to the balance which the decision maker has struck between different rights, as well as assessing the relative weight given to interests and considerations in a particular case. It is a good idea to take this into account in your decision making process.

2.79 Go back to the aim that was given as the answers to questions **1.2**, **4.2** and perhaps also question **3.1**. Are the reasons for needing the policy good strong ones? And is the action proposed the only way of achieving the aim? Is there any other way that you can think of which would allow you to meet the aim but would not require you to restrict people's rights? If there is, note it here.

2.80 If there is an alternative way of achieving the aim, and your organisation decides not to adopt it, you will need to set out the reasons for this decision. The reasons will need to be good ones. They might include either human resources or financial resources. Or if it is necessary to ensure that other people's fundamental rights are protected, you might not be sure that your alternative method will achieve this outcome. However, you should show that it has been considered.

2.81 Think too about the right that is being restricted. What will the restrictions take away from this right? Will there be anything left of it? The examples below should help you.

Case illustrations: restricting rights – is it proportionate?

The Prison Service separates mothers and babies after the children reach the age of 18 months. Two mothers challenged this policy in court claiming that their article 8 rights were in question. The court said that the interests of the child must be more important than the interests of the mother in these cases: they were therefore most concerned with the child's article 8 rights. However, the court also had to decide whether the Prison Service could operate its policy in such a rigid way, with no flexibility. The judges found that one of the mothers should win her case. There was a potential for harm to the child, there was no plan for the child's future, and the judges believed that the harm the prison might do the child would be less than the harm of separation. They asked the Prison Service to think again, and be more flexible.

An adoption agency had a policy that it would never disclose adoption records to people who had been adopted. A woman challenged this decision. She had been adopted when she was 2 years old. Her adoptive parents had died, and her only living relatives were her birth mother's younger sisters, and two half sisters of her genetic father. She had seen some of the documents from her file, and wanted to see the rest. She believed that her article 8 rights were being violated. The court found that the adoption agency should have looked at each document individually, rather than applying a blanket policy and that the adoption agency must look again at its policy and see if it fits modern standards of disclosure. The judges also said that the adoption agency did not give enough thought to the specific facts relating to the individual concerned – particularly the fact that others who might have wanted things to continue to be secret had died. Although they considered Human Rights Act arguments, the judges felt they would have given the same judgment even without the HRA in place.

A single mother with three young children had lived for seven years in a London borough, waiting for a decision on her asylum status. Finally she was granted asylum. The London borough placed her in temporary bed and breakfast accommodation in Birmingham. The woman could speak very little English and had no family or friends in Birmingham.
Her children had to move schools and the move disrupted medical treatment for one of the children who had a broken collarbone. The move meant that her former partner could not see his children. The council said that the accommodation was only temporary and that their decision was reasonable. The courts disagreed. The judges said they were wrong to ask the woman to move to Birmingham. The council knew about her circumstances, and they also knew that she would be in the bed and breakfast accommodation for a much longer time than the word 'temporary' would imply. The local authority's decision breached her article 8 rights and the court said that the woman's application for housing must be heard within 21 days of the case ending.

Local authorities sell the data that they collect for the electoral roll to commercial organisations who use it for marketing purposes. A man who brought a case to court thought that it was wrong that his right to vote (article 3 protocol 1) depended upon his information being passed on to others. His only option to prevent this was to stay off the electoral roll. The court agreed. They said that because people are not able to object to their data being passed on to third parties, there is a disproportionate restriction on the right to vote. The way in which the electoral roll data is collected and used has changed because of this case. Residents now have the ability to opt out of the register that can be sold to third parties.

4.6 Think about the diversity of clients, staff and service users that your organisation works with. Would the answer to question 2.2 be different if considered from another perspective? If so, how?

2.82   The answer to question **2.2** will have identified the rights that your policy or procedure might impact upon. Could the answer to this question be different if you considered it from the perspective of a particular group of service users, clients or others whose rights might be affected? In other words, could the policy have a differential impact if considered from a broader perspective? Could it discriminate – perhaps unintentionally – against a particular group of people?

2.83   If there is a differential impact, and a particular group of clients, service users, or other people could be particularly affected by your policy, work through the mini checklist specifically related to article 14 in chapter 4 below. Restrictions on rights should not discriminate unless this can be justified. Remember that the Human Rights Act defines discrimination broadly. It doesn't just talk about race, sex and colour – but also about language, religion, and 'other status'. Also remember that 'other status' can include age, sexuality and disability.

Section five – organisational process

5.1   Who has been consulted about this policy or procedure?

5.2   Who must agree to the policy or procedure before it can be finalised?

5.3   How will people get the training and information they need to ensure that the policy or procedure works?

2.84   This section provides an opportunity to check that you have covered all the organisational aspects of the policy and that you are happy with the advice that you have taken so far. After completing these questions you may decide to consult more widely outside your team, department or organisation. This can be helpful – it might enable your organisation to become aware of any unforeseen Human Rights Act implications and to amend the policy or procedure accordingly. It can be particularly useful to get a fresh perspective on issues to which you have become close. Broader consultation also provides you with an opportunity to get any specialist or legal help or advice that you need.

2.85   Staff will need to be provided with the training and support that they need to put the policy into practice in a way that will ensure the Human Rights Act aspects of it are met. If private contractors or charities are involved in the delivery of your policy or service, they will need to understand their responsibilities under the Human Rights Act. These can be set out contractually, in the same way as any other issues, although it might be wise to ensure that third parties are really aware of the implications of such a clause.

2.86   If aspects of the policy are still unclear or you are unsure whether it is compliant with the Human Rights Act, now is the time to seek advice from a line manager, or from the legal department or an appropriate solicitor. Even if a policy has been reviewed since October 2000 when the Human Rights Act came into force more recent case law may provide you with better information.

2.87   The checklist is now complete. If your review process identified an impact on article 6 rights or article 14 rights, there are two separate mini checklists that can be completed to help you understand these areas in more detail.

Mini checklist: the right to a fair trial

Mini checklist

1   Does the policy or decision impact on someone's civil rights – and if so, what are these?

2   What kind of appeal process exists if someone disagrees with the decision?

3   Does the decision making process allow the person access to a court to challenge the decision at some stage during the process?

4   Does the individual whose rights are affected have the ability to participate in the decision making process at some stage? If not, are the reasons for this likely to be considered necessary under the Human Rights Act?

5   Is the person whose rights are affected provided with the reasons for the decision when it is made? If not, can the decision making process be amended so that it is possible?

6   Is there a review process that can scrutinise the decision? If so, is the tribunal or review panel independent, and operating within the relevant human rights principles?

3.29   Article 6 and public consultation

7   Does the consultation process take into account the relevant article 6 principles?

8   Does the process range as widely as possible amongst a cross-section of people that might be affected by the decision?

9   Does the consultation process give people the opportunity to understand the reasons for the decision that is taken at the end of the process?

Introduction

3.1 This mini checklist will help assess the impact of any policies or procedures in relation to article 6 of the European Convention on Human Rights, brought into British law through the Human Rights Act. Article 6 is often known in shorthand as 'the right to a fair trial'. However, it is important to remember that this article applies to what are known as *civil matters* as well as criminal proceedings.

3.2 Many of the principles that are covered through using this mini checklist are common sense. Some people would describe them as the principles of natural justice, others as procedural fairness. Still, it is sensible to make sure that they have been explicitly considered and a Human Rights Act framework is helpful because it allows these key principles to be drawn out.

3.3 These principles have to be complied with *at some stage* in the process, though not at every stage. In many cases, people whose rights are affected will have the ability to challenge decisions in court. If that is the case, it is the court hearing that guarantees the right to a fair trial but even if decisions can be challenged in court, it is good practice to build article 6 principles into the decision making process at an early stage. In some cases, this may ensure that people feel fairly treated from the start, preventing the need for court cases. Avoiding a court case is obviously much cheaper for your organisation in the long-term, as it takes up less staff time and avoids any damage to your organisation's reputation.

3.4 This mini checklist is divided into two sections. The first relates to making a decision that affects someone's civil rights, and works through a series of important principles. It can be used to inform good practice in an existing process or when setting up a new process that will determine someone's rights. It refers both to decisions that might be made by officers or staff within an organisation, and to an appeal panel or tribunal if one exists. It might also inform good practice in drafting internal complaints procedures, for example in residential accommodation. Procedural fairness is particularly important in decisions that relate to a person's home, family, or property rights and some extra information about these areas is included.

3.5 The second section relates to public consultation. This includes instances when the final decision could have a direct impact on someone's human rights – such as housing transfer. Article 6 principles can provide good practice that can help in designing a public consultation process on a range of issues, particularly those that might have an impact on the local environment. A thorough and open consultation process can help your organisation to defend itself if a decision is later challenged in court, perhaps through judicial review.

Why is article 6 important?

3.6   Fairness in decision making procedures is a vital principle in protecting people's human rights. If the decision making process is unfair, open to undue influence, or allows the making of arbitrary decisions, people's rights can be affected. Principles such as access to proceedings, disclosure of documents, and the ability to cross examine witnesses and put another side of the story are important because they open up processes to scrutiny. For this reason, the way in which decisions are made can be as important as the final decision.

3.7   Evidence that the type of framework set out in this mini checklist has been followed could help you or your organisation to demonstrate, if challenged, that you were aware of people's article 6 rights, and wanted to uphold them in the process, even if the subsequent decision means that other human rights are affected. For example, a planning decision that leads to compulsory purchase of properties could have an impact on some residents' right to enjoy their possessions, protected by article 1, protocol 1. However, if the consultation process was fair and open you will be able to demonstrate respect for their right to a fair hearing in the determination of their other rights.

What are civil rights?

3.8   Civil rights and obligations is a phrase that is used to cover a wide range of activities. It includes issues between private individuals that could be settled at court under civil law such as the law of contract, employment law, and property law. It also includes damages, and the enforcement of judgments. It can also include much of the interaction between individuals and public bodies. Part II of the *Human Rights Act Toolkit* contains more information about this area.

3.9   In some situations public bodies will have legal responsibilities relating to the civil rights of individuals – for example to provide housing, or benefits, or to uphold trading standards. In such cases, article 6 is a very important area to consider in the decision making process. At other times, the responsibilities that a public authority has may be discretionary: people may believe that they should get access to particular benefits or rights, but there is nothing in the law to say that this is the case. Things like non-obligatory payments or discretionary benefits or payments – because they are not a right in law – would not under current case law fall within the scope of article 6. Your organisation should have already made it clear whether or not your work could be classed as determining people's civil rights and obligations.

3.10   Broadly speaking decisions affecting the following areas have been regarded as affecting people's civil rights:

- welfare benefit claims including some asylum support claims, (particularly the withdrawal of support);
- disciplinary proceedings in relation to professional standing that will decide whether a person can continue to practice their profession;
- property disputes (including planning);
- housing;
- licensing decisions (whether commercial or professional);
- surveillance affecting people's ability to trade or practice their profession;
- child care – including adoption, fostering and children at risk;
- compensation issues – where the compensation would be paid by the public authority as a result of their failure to uphold proper standards.

3.11   It is important to remember that case law is changing all the time in this area. When making decisions that affect people's lives, it is good practice to rely on article 6 principles – whatever the area of work.

If I don't deal with civil rights issues – do I need to know?

3.12   Yes. It's dangerous simply to decide that your work, or that of your organisation, doesn't need to comply with article 6 principles because it's such a broad area. Following article 6 principles can demonstrate good practice in decision making. Clients may increasingly come to expect this in any case because of their interaction with other public bodies. In addition, if the decision itself is subsequently challenged using other sections of the Human Rights Act, evidence that article 6 principles have been followed may help your organisation's case in court. These principles can also be useful in designing a consultation process covering issues which are not of themselves civil rights issues but which might be covered by other parts of the Human Rights Act, or which could come under scrutiny in the courts.

3.13   So this mini checklist is also important in relation to:

- housing registers – including allocations and transfers;
- housing decisions – where your organisation is acting as landlord;
- school exclusions – including Independent Appeal Panels;
- school admissions;
- community care – including residential care charges; and
- residential care homes.

3.14   In some cases, as you can see from the next case illustration, the courts may rely on Human Rights Act arguments, even though those bringing or defending the case do not raise them. Courts and tribunals are able to do this because they too are public authorities under the Human Rights Act. This is another good reason to ensure that human rights arguments are taken into account in a decision making process.

Case illustrations: court use of Human Rights Act arguments

A pawnbroker took a client to court to try to enforce an incorrectly drafted agreement and reclaim money that he had lent. Neither the pawnbroker nor the woman who had been lent the money used the Human Rights Act in the case. But the courts did. They said that the Consumer Credit Act 1974 contained sections that are incompatible with the Human Rights Act. These sections denied the lender the right to go to court to enforce payment of the debt. The court felt this did not give the right balance of rights and denied the pawnbroker the ability to enjoy his possessions (article 1, protocol 1).

A mother had put her baby up for adoption. The father wanted to adopt the child. The mother and the social work team were happy with the arrangement even though it meant that the child would have had no, or little, contact with the mother after the adoption had taken place. None of the people involved in the case referred to the Human Rights Act but the court was not happy and after an appeal it used the Human Rights Act to say why. The court felt that it was not in the child's interests to have its mother excluded from its life at such an early age and that the adoption order was disproportionate. The judges said that article 8 of the Convention meant that the relationship between mother and child of itself was 'family life'. So instead of granting the adoption order, the courts gave a residence order until the child was 18.

Mini checklist

1   Does the policy or decision impact on someone's civil rights – and if so, what are these?

2   What kind of appeal process exists if someone disagrees with the decision?

3   Does the decision making process allow the person access to a court to challenge the decision at some stage during the process?

3.15   The first three questions in this section are introductory. They will provide clarity about the context within which decisions are made. If the decision has an impact on people's civil rights and your organisation has already provided you with guidance, note it here. If it does not, and you simply want to ensure that you comply with good practice, you should note this too. If in doubt, seek advice from your manager, or from the legal team or department.

3.16   Note the types of appeal mechanisms that are available to people to allow them to challenge your decision. Article 6 principles do not need to apply at every stage in the process (though it is good practice to apply as many as possible from an early stage). If the decision can be reviewed by an independent body you may want to ensure that this body complies with article 6 principles as far as is possible although this is not strictly necessary if the decision can be challenged in court at a later stage.

3.17   If the decision can be challenged in a court or a tribunal that is part of the legal system it is this part of the process that will act as the 'guarantee' for people's article 6 rights.

4   Does the individual whose rights are affected have the ability to participate in the decision making process at some stage? If not, are the reasons for this likely to be considered necessary under the Human Rights Act?

3.18   Article 6 principles are concerned with ensuring that the decision making process is as fair as possible, and that the person whose rights will be affected has the opportunity to participate in the process. Another term for this is procedural fairness.

3.19   Many of the following principles that need to be considered will already be part of the decision making process. This section makes them explicit and ensures that they are considered. These principles should all be met *at some stage* during the decision making process. If a review tribunal exists or the decision can be challenged in court, it is not necessary for all of these provisions to be met at a very early stage. However, it is good practice to ensure that staff or officers making decisions about people's rights work to these standards as much as possible since this may prevent a subsequent legal challenge. This is particularly important if the decision impacts upon people's article 8 rights to respect for their private and family life or their home, or to their rights to property under article 1 of protocol 1.

3.20   Consider the following points, and assess whether the process you have in place meets these standards.

- The person whose rights will be affected has the right to *an independent and impartial tribunal*. If staff make initial decisions, there must be an ability for the person to ask an independent body to reconsider these, perhaps through an oversight panel, or ultimately to a court or tribunal.
- The person whose rights will be affected has the *ability to be present* at some stage during the decision making process (though this can be restricted).
- The person whose rights will be affected should be given a reasonable opportunity to *present their case* before the decision is made. This opportunity should be in a situation that does not put them at a disadvantage to their opponent, and the case that they make should be considered before a decision is made.

- The person whose rights will be affected has the right to *an adversarial hearing*. This means that they can see and know what others have said, challenge any inaccuracies that exist through cross-examination, and address the decision making panel themselves.
- The person whose rights will be affected has the right to *disclosure* of all relevant documents – and the ability to comment on these, particularly in cases of disagreement. They should receive any relevant documents before a hearing takes place so that they have time to think.
- The hearing that will make the decision about their rights should take place within a *reasonable time*. The phrase 'a reasonable time' may mean different things to decision makers and those whose rights are affected.

3.21   If the process does not comply with these principles they can be used as good practice to improve it. If at a later stage the person whose rights are affected has the ability to appeal to a tribunal or review panel that does comply with these principles, note this here.

3.22   The issue of procedural fairness is particularly important in the case of decisions that relate to someone's family life, their right to a home, or their right to protection for their property. If decision making will involve these areas extra care is needed. The following points should be noted:

- The courts have decided that 'respect for family life' will only be a reality if the interests of family members are taken into account when decisions are made. It is particularly important that the interests of the parents are considered if the case involves a care, access or custody decision.
- Disclosure is also very important in decisions relating to family matters. If parents don't have the information on which a decision is based, they can't participate properly. Information should be disclosed to parents from the very start of the process.
- In making decisions about a person's right to a home, the courts use procedural fairness to help them decide whether the eventual outcome is 'necessary and proportionate'. The involvement of the person concerned is particularly important if the decision has an impact on their family.
- When decisions relate to property, it is particularly important that the person affected has an opportunity to challenge the decision that has been made before their property is taken from them. This helps to provide the 'fair balance' that the article promises to protect.

Case illustrations – article 6 standards in action

The courts found that part of the Mental Health Act 1983 was incompatible with the Human Rights Act. Patients who were detained in hospital under this law used to have to prove to the Mental Health Review Tribunal that they should be released. The courts said that the burden of proof should not rest with the patient. Instead it should be for the Tribunal to be sure that the patient's detention is justified if release is refused. This ensures that the burden of proof meets article 6 standards. Because of the court's decision, the Mental Health Act had to be changed by Parliament.

The courts have decided that someone who has a disability does not receive a fair trial if the judge does not take their disability into account. In one particular case, the person was required to carry on with their case until late into the afternoon, when this was difficult for them, and meant that they were exhausted. This put them at a disadvantage and did not meet article 6 standards.

A solicitor was reported to the Office for the Supervision of Solicitors and struck off the Roll of Solicitors for conduct unbefitting a solicitor. He was not present at the hearing, and no one represented him. He said this was unfair. The courts looked at the procedure as a whole and found that it was not. They said that the solicitor had known about the case for a long time, had plenty of opportunity to tell the hearing of his defence, and that as he was an experienced solicitor he could have been expected to participate himself, without representation. They found that in this case his article 6 rights were not breached.

An Employment Tribunal was due to hear a case of sex and race discrimination. The man whose case was to be heard was ill, and faxed a letter to the tribunal, with a medical certificate, asking for the case to be adjourned until he was well enough to attend. The chair of the tribunal decided that the case would go ahead, despite receiving a second medical certificate. When the case came before the tribunal, the complaint was dismissed because the man was not present to make his case. The courts found that this was wrong. The tribunal did not tell the man why they had decided to go ahead, and made no reference to the reasons why they had ignored his letter and medical evidence. This did not comply with article 6 standards. So, the courts found that the man had been denied his right to a fair trial.

Two motorists believed that their right to silence was an absolute right and could not be restricted. They had both been caught on speed cameras, driving above the speed limit, and had been fined and given penalty points. One was driving at 69 mph in a restricted 40 mph area of the M11. The other was driving at 47 mph in a 30 mph zone. Both said that because they had been sent a Notice of Intended Prosecution asking them to provide the full name and address of the driver at the time and occasion specified in the notice, their human rights had been violated. The human rights organisation Liberty agreed and supported their case to the European Court of Human Rights. Fortunately the court did not agree. The judges in Europe's highest court decided, by 13 votes to 2, that because only limited information was sought by the notice, and because it was restricted to a regulatory regime for motor vehicles, the 'essence' of the men's right to remain silent had not been destroyed. The court said that as the possession of cars was recognised to have the potential to cause grave injury those who chose to drive 'have accepted certain responsibilities and obligations ... in the legal framework of the United Kingdom these responsibilities include the obligation in the event of suspected road traffic offences to inform the authorities of the identity of the driver'. So asking car owners to tell the authorities who was driving if their car is caught exceeding the speed limit does meet the standards set by article 6.

5   Is the person whose rights are affected provided with the reasons for the decision when it is made? If not, can the decision making process be amended so that this is possible?

3.23   This question focuses on the type of reasons that a person whose rights are affected might be given to enable them to understand the decision that has been made. If a person understands the reason for a decision they will be better placed to challenge it if they believe that it is wrong, so the provision of reasons is an important human rights principle. In addition, providing reasons demonstrates that the person's own individual case has been considered, rather than the decision making process simply applying a blanket policy with no consideration of the individual's specific needs.

3.24   Sometimes decision making processes can be very complex. It is not necessary for the person to be given lengthy and detailed responses to every point that has been raised. A simple explanation of the main reasons for making the decision will be adequate.

3.25   If the decision making process does not give reasons for the decisions it would be wise to amend it so that it does. Note suggestions here and discuss these with colleagues, or seek further legal advice.

6   Is there a review process that can scrutinise the decision? If so, is the tribunal or review panel independent, and operating within the relevant human rights principles?

3.26   To meet article 6 principles it is necessary to provide the person whose rights have been affected with the ability to have your decision reviewed. This review may be carried out by a tribunal, review panel or other independent body, or by the courts themselves. In some cases, both of these processes will exist. If the review body, tribunal or appeal panel is managed or serviced by you or your colleagues, you may want to assess whether it complies with human rights principles and suggest changes to make it more compliant. Of course, it is the courts that will provide the final guarantee of compliance with article 6 rights, so it may not be strictly necessary for bodies at a lower level to comply with article 6 in full. However, it is sensible to take account of these principles as far as is possible. If a legal challenge is subsequently brought, the body's decision is less likely to be overturned on the grounds that the process of decision making was flawed if there is compliance at an early stage with article 6.

3.27   The independence and impartiality of a tribunal, appeal panel or review body (the body) is very important. Human rights principles when applied to this area cover a number of issues and you should consider each of these in turn. If it becomes clear that the decision making processes do not meet these standards, make the body aware of your concerns. It may be necessary to reconsider their working arrangements.

3.28   The tribunal, appeal panel or review body must be:

- Able to take *binding decisions*. It must be able to do more than give advice, or to recommend that the original decision makers think again. If necessary, it must be able to look at the facts and overturn the initial decision. A body that can only consider the decision making process, rather than reviewing the facts, is unlikely to be considered adequate under human rights standards.

- *Independent*. Its members should be appointed on terms that allow them to act independently, free from the fear that their appointment may be affected by the decisions that they make. The body must not just be independent – it must *be seen to be independent*. It may be easier to demonstrate this if lay people, or people from outside a specialist field are involved in the process, as well as those with professional knowledge. If a panel follows guidance issued by the government, for example in the case of panels considering school exclusions, it must treat the guidance as just that, and not rely upon it as a set of rigid rules.

- *Free from conflicts of interest*. If the decision making process might in some way affect individual members of the body, or their organisation, they should not be involved in hearing an appeal or complaint.

- Run in a way that *ensures independence from those who made the initial decision*. Where staff or officers are presenting evidence to the body, they should avoid presenting recommendations for action at the same time. Staff or officers should also be available for questioning by the body if necessary. Staff or officers should withdraw from the room when a decision is being made, and should not be able to vote.

- Capable of providing a *public hearing*. In some cases this will be unnecessary or undesirable – for example in cases involving children. In others, even if a body can sit in public, the individual concerned may ask for a private hearing. If the decision that the review body makes can be appealed directly to a court, the right to a public hearing will be met at this stage.

Capable of providing *reasons* for its decision. These need not be lengthy and detailed – a simple explanation of the main points of the decision will be adequate.

Case illustrations – independence of decision making bodies

A Housing Benefit Review Board considered a claimant's case. They decided he was not entitled to housing benefit. The man asked for the decision to be reviewed. The Chair of the Review Board, and two other members, also sat as elected councillors for the local council that would have to pay him the benefit. The claimant said the tribunal was not independent. The court agreed. It said that the councillors were too closely connected to the local authority (and the local authority did not want to have to pay the benefit). Though the procedure was fair, the people judging it were not independent.

In Scotland a man brought a case against the Temporary Sheriffs system. Temporary Sheriffs were appointed for one year, usually on a renewable contract. The man thought this meant the Temporary Sheriff could not make an independent decision in his case. The judge agreed. He thought that this was a 'career move' post, too dependent on re-appointment, and the person holding it would not feel confident in their ability to make decisions. He felt that this was not compatible with independence, nor did it look independent to an outsider.

A woman belonged to the Kennel Club. She was convicted of 16 offences under the Protection of Animals Act, and after her conviction the Kennel Club committee met to decide what to do in her case. They decided to ban her for five years – which would prevent her from working anywhere in the world. She was not at the hearing, which was held in private and she had no right of appeal; she said this was unfair. The court disagreed. They said that she had already received a public hearing – a criminal trial – and so no other hearing was necessary. The court also said that the person who told the committee about the facts in her case did not have a vote on the final decision. So, the committee was independent. The court did find that the penalty was disproportionate however, and it changed it to a shorter ban.

A number of children who had been permanently excluded from school brought a case against their local authority. Lawyers for the children said that the Independent Appeal

> Panels were not independent because they had considered themselves to be bound by the guidance issued by the Education Secretary. The courts found that in this case the guidance was acceptable but the judge said that panels following guidance 'must keep in mind that guidance is no more than that: it is not direction and certainly not rules.' Independent panels, the judge said, had to exercise their own judgment, whilst taking the guidance into account.

Article 6 and public consultation

3.29 Article 6 principles can also be useful when designing and implementing a consultation process, whether the process relates to a decision (for example, around planning or licensing) or the design of a new policy. The questions below apply article 6 principles to the consultation processes. In some cases the application of article 6 principles is good practice. In others, involving article 8 or article 1, protocol 1 rights, it is necessary and particularly important to explicitly consider article 6 to ensure procedural fairness.

7   Does the consultation process take account of the relevant article 6 principles?

3.30 Article 6 principles can be very useful in helping to shape the way in which a consultation process is run. They can help to demonstrate, if there is a subsequent challenge, that the consultation process complied with human rights standards by thoroughly reviewing all the facts. The more thorough the consultation process is, the more likely it is that this can be demonstrated. In many cases, a challenge to this type of process will come through judicial review. It used to be the case that judicial review could only really examine the decision making process. However, because of the Human Rights Act many judicial review hearings are now examining the facts of the case – the reasons for the decision – as well as the way in which the decision has been made. So the consultation process will need to allow for decision makers to do the same.

3.31 If the decision is likely to deprive people of their property, for example through compulsory purchase, a thorough consultation process may be particularly important. Your organisation may be a significant beneficiary – for example through planning gain – if a decision is agreed. In this case, it may be sensible to appoint an independent panel to help you run the consultation process. This can provide an extra guarantee of both independence and transparency. In the case of a later legal challenge this may be important.

3.32   A consultation process shaped by article 6 principles will:

- Provide people with the *ability to participate* by making it clear how the decision will be made and on what grounds, setting out the type of evidence that will be accepted and timetabling opportunities for participation. It is acceptable to limit participation to those who will be affected by the decision, such as local residents.
- Work to *reasonable timescales,* allowing people time to put arguments together and to find out facts.
- Allow people *reasonable access* to documents that are submitted as part of the consultation process, unless there are necessary reasons (for example, on security grounds) why this might not be possible.
- Hold *hearings in public* and allow *people to question evidence* that is given as part of the process.
- Ensure that any review group or body running the consultation process is *appointed in a transparent manner,* and has terms and conditions that guarantee its independence.
- Be at a time when the proposals that are being considered are *still at a formative stage* – not when they have been decided.

Case illustrations – consultation processes and the Human Rights Act

Some local residents who live near Heathrow Airport took the British government to the European Court of Human Rights. They said that the noise level in their homes caused by night flights was affecting their sleep. At first the courts said that the government had not considered the right balance between the rights of individuals (particularly respect for their private and family life protected by article 8) and the public interest when they thought about a flight control system. For example they did not carry out their own research into the reality of commercial benefits of night flights – they simply relied on what they were told by others. Nor did they conduct a complete study on the effects of aircraft noise on sleep prevention – though they had looked at sleep disturbance. Given the lack of evidence on these two points, the court agreed with the local residents, and found that the government had violated their article 8 rights. But the government appealed the case to a higher court, the Grand Chamber, and this time it won by 12 votes to 5. The government told the courts that it was about to give residents the opportunity to give their views on night flights in a new consultation. The court found that the economic benefits of night flights from the airport outweighed the human rights of those whose sleep was disturbed because they lived on the flight path. The court also found that there had been no impact on property values in the area, which meant that if people wanted to move away, they could do so without penalty. The Grand Chamber took back the damages that local residents had won – around £4,000 each. But the court did find that the government had failed to give local residents and the three local authorities supporting the campaign a fair hearing in British courts.

A local authority wanted to close two care homes for older people. The local authority wrote to all residents, to say that it wanted to make changes to the way in which it provided care. It said there would be a full consultation with service users and their families. After a whole series of meetings, the council's Scrutiny and Review Panel met. Members of the panel had a detailed report that had not been provided to residents, though a copy of the report was available in the council's library. The report said that there was a structural fault in one of the buildings that the council wanted to close. This was not true, as the solicitor for the residents discovered. The judge found that the time period for consultation – two months – had put residents and relatives under considerable pressure. He was also unhappy with the way in which the reasons for closing the homes had been presented, since one of the reasons given was incorrect or misleading. The judge also felt the discussion of policy considerations relating to the closure was very brief, and no alternatives to closure were suggested. This meant that the consultation process did not operate fairly, and was not meaningful. The judge also found that there was no evidence to show that the council had considered the article 8 rights of the residents in any way, and so closing the home, which would be a clear interference with article 8 rights could not be justified. He ordered the council to reconsider the matter again, to consult the residents properly and to consider their article 8 rights.

8   Does the process range as widely as possible amongst a cross-section of people that might be affected by the decision?

3.33   Thinking through at an early stage the groups of people that might be affected by your decision can help to assess whether there are any particular groups whose views need to be heard but who might not usually respond to consultations. Thinking this through now will help at a later stage if there is a need to demonstrate that no-one has been discriminated against because of their status. If you would like more information about this area, read the mini checklist for article 14 in the next chapter. You will also need to make sure you comply with any obligation to promote equality that may be imposed by the Disability Equality Duty, the Gender Equality Duty, or the Race Relations (Amendment) Act.

3.34   Remember that some groups of people may be affected by the eventual decision but find it hard to participate in the consultation. So it might be necessary to demonstrate that consideration has been given to how people's different needs might be met during the process.

9   Does the consultation process give people the opportunity to understand the reasons for the decision that is taken at the end of the process?

3.35   Once a consultation process has been conducted, and a decision made, it is good practice if using article 6 principles to provide reasons for the decision. It may be particularly important to provide the reasons for the decision to those who participated in the consultation process in case they wish to challenge it. There is no need to provide a lengthy and detailed answer to every question raised during the process: a simple explanation of the main reasons for the decision will be adequate.

Mini checklist: discrimination

Mini checklist

1   Could the decision constitute differential treatment?

2   If there is differential treatment, is it justified? If yes, explain this

3   If there is differential treatment, is the policy proportionate to the outcome that it will produce? Explain how this is so

4   What would lessen the disproportionate impact?

5   If this alternative has been rejected, what are the reasons?

4.20   Communicating the decision

6   Is there a particular group of people that would find it difficult to find out about the way in which the policy or decision might impact on their rights? Who?

7   How can it be made clear to this group of people how their rights might be affected?

8   If the restriction on rights is a response to an individual's behaviour or conduct, how can this be communicated effectively to all likely to be affected?

Introduction

4.1   This mini checklist relates to article 14 of the European Convention on Human Rights, brought into UK law through the Human Rights Act. Remember that this article of the Convention does not stand on its own. It can only be linked to another right protected by the Human Rights Act.

4.2   If you simply want to ensure that your existing good practice in relation to anti-discrimination processes and procedures is keeping up with the changes that the Human Rights Act may bring, this checklist can be used on its own.

Why is there a separate checklist on discrimination?

4.3   UK law already contains a number of anti-discrimination laws, such as the Race Relations Act 1976, the Disability Discrimination Act 1995, the Sex Discrimination Act 1970, and the newer laws which place a responsibility on the public sector to prevent discrimination and promote equality: the Disability Equality Duty, the Gender Equality Duty and the Race Relations (Amendment) Act 2000. There are also other laws which act to create a level playing field between individuals that people don't immediately think of as being about equality – such as the Rehabilitation of Offenders Act 1974. The Human Rights Act is different.

4.4   The first thing to remember is that the text of article 14 is drawn much more widely than existing equality laws. Look at the text below:

> The enjoyment of the rights and freedoms set forth in this Convention shall be secured without discrimination on any ground such as sex, race, colour, language, religion, political or other opinion, national or social origin, association with a national minority, property, birth or other status.

4.5   The words 'such as' and 'other status' are important. Do not assume that because something does not appear in this list, it does not matter. These words are important in opening up the grounds on which people may experience discrimination. This list should be treated as a starting point.

4.6   The reason for this is straightforward. Stopping discrimination is a very important principle in human rights thinking, based on the premise that every human being deserves equal respect simply *because they are a human being.* There are other international human rights documents that talk about this in more detail in relation to race, gender and disability, as well as from a children's perspective.

4.7 The meaning of the word discrimination is an important concept within the legal judgments under the Convention. Discrimination is taken to mean a *difference in treatment that has no reasonable and objective justification.* From this definition it is obvious that sometimes you are able to discriminate – in fact sometimes it may be desirable. The checklist will help explain in more detail when you can, and when you cannot, discriminate against particular groups of people by treating them differently.

4.8 Treating people differently – *or differential treatment* as it is known under the Human Rights Act – can mean two things.

- Treating people in the same situation differently because of their status, or;
- treating people in a different situation – who have different needs – in the same way, regardless of those needs.

Mini checklist

The decision

1 Could the decision constitute differential treatment?

4.9 This question is straightforward. Consider whether the decision that will be made could lead to some form of differential treatment. Start by reading article 14 again, thinking about the list of groups of people that it includes. However, think more broadly about whether there are any other groups of people that the decision might impact upon in a way that would cause differential treatment. As an example, we know through legal judgments that the term 'other status' includes sexuality, disability, professional status, imprisonment and marital status. The case illustrations that follow this question show three examples of differential treatment.

4.10 Remember that differential treatment doesn't have to involve treating people differently. It can include treating people with very different needs in the same way – and thus not recognising their individual human rights. If the answer to this question is 'yes', it will help to also note the discrimination that has been identified.

Case illustrations: differential treatment

A large comprehensive school in a UK city is reviewing its exclusions policy. It has become clear that either the policy itself, or the way in which the policy is being applied, is having unintended consequences. A report to the head teacher and governors shows that in the last 6 months, 25 children have been excluded from school. 24 of them are Asian, 1 is white and all are boys. In the last 6 months, another 14 pupils have been given a warning about their conduct. 10 of them are white, 2 Black and 2 Asian; 11 are girls. In some cases, pupils have been given warnings for their behaviour when others have been excluded in very similar circumstances. The school is concerned that their policy is being applied in a way that leads to pupils in the same situation being treated differently because of their status, and worried that this will lead to a challenge under the Human Rights Act. The school governors decide that while a strong exclusions policy is necessary to enable all children in the school to enjoy a right to an education (itself covered by the Human Rights Act), they need to take further action to make sure the policy is not applied in a way that breaches article 14 of the Convention when put together with the right to an education – article 2, protocol 1.

The maternity department in a busy inner-city hospital has many women who come for ante-natal appointments whose first language is not English. Staff are concerned that some of these women don't really understand what is said to them, which could be dangerous. These mothers may also miss out on other information that's available about benefits, childcare, and healthcare for a new baby. The hospital listens to the staff concerns and sets up an interpreting/advocacy service. However the booking system automatically allocates the same length appointments for all patients. This isn't long enough for patients using the advocacy service, who need more time. The hospital refuses to change the booking system, saying that other mothers will ask why they don't get longer with the doctors. Some of the staff team suggest that this treats women who have very different needs as if they are all the same, and could breach the Human Rights Act in relation to articles 8 and 14.

During the late 1960s after a period of political turmoil in Africa, British passport holders tried to come to England – as they had the legal right to do – to start a new life. Many of them were East African Asians, fleeing persecution in Kenya, Tanzania and Uganda. The British government changed the law to try and prevent them from settling in the UK. Asian people in Africa already faced destitution. When they arrived in the UK, unnecessary immigration controls meant that they were moved around the country from one place to another, making their situation worse. Some of the families concerned challenged the British government's decision in the European Court of Human Rights. The Court found that the British government's policy institutionalised racist practices. They ruled that it was discriminatory, degrading and that it violated the article 3 rights of these British passport holders. The Court said 'publicly to single out a group of persons for differential treatment on the basis of race might, in certain circumstances, constitute a special form of affront to human dignity.'

4.11 The next questions will help to assess whether the decision that is to be made can be justified in a way that will meet human rights standards. For this to happen it must be possible to show that the differential treatment proposed has a reasonable and objective justification. This will require facts and a body of evidence to support your case. If you don't have such evidence, you will need either to find it, or to think again about the proposal. The questions below expand on this in more detail.

2   If there is differential treatment, is it justified? If yes, explain this.

4.12 First, ask yourself if the policy has a *legitimate aim*. Another way to think about this is to ask whether the policy is really designed to be administratively convenient, rather than to benefit the users or clients. Are service users' needs at the heart of the policy – or has practice adapted over time to make it easier or more convenient for staff to carry out their jobs? If this is the case, it may not have a legitimate aim. An example of administrative convenience is shown in the following case illustration. If it seems that the policy has a legitimate aim, move on.

Case illustration: administrative convenience

In the past people who had been detained under the Mental Health Act but who disagreed with this decision had to wait at least eight weeks before their appeal against detention could be heard by a Mental Health Review Tribunal. For someone detained against their will who thought that their detention was wrong, this was a long time to wait. This eight-week wait was challenged using the Human Rights Act, relying on the right to liberty and security which entitles people to have their case heard within reasonable time. The judge found that the eight-week time limit could not be justified in every case and that it was a policy that suited the administrative staff rather than people who had been detained. Sometimes a case might need a longer time limit to prepare material, but often cases could be heard much more quickly. He said that the eight-week time limit was 'bred in the bone of administrative convenience, not administrative necessity'. His decision overturned an administrative practice within the tribunal system that had been in place for many years.

---

3   If there is differential treatment, is the policy proportionate to the outcome that it will produce? Explain how this is so.

4.13   This question asks about an important principle that you will have already come across earlier in the *Toolkit* – that of proportionality. Is the difference in treatment that is proposed proportionate in its outcome? A number of things need to be demonstrated in relation to this question. It is important to note that if the policy discriminates against people because of their race, religion, nationality, or gender the reasons presented will need to be strong and compelling.

4.14   Firstly, think about whether there really are a number of relevant reasons that support the difference in treatment. Is there objective evidence to show that the policy can be justified? That is likely to mean facts, not opinions. If there is no such evidence it will need to be found, or the policy will need to be reconsidered.

4.15   Secondly, consider the impact of the policy on the individuals that you believe it may discriminate against. Consider not only the outcome that the policy is intended to have but also any outcomes that may be unintended. They may perhaps be beyond your organisation's control – but if the policy contributes to them, you may need to show that you have thought about them at an early stage. If an unintended outcome is identified at this point it may be wise to reconsider the policy.

4.16   Finally, think about whether the policy is intended to compensate for years of inequality in the past and could constitute *positive action*. You may know this intention by its legal name of *positive discrimination*. Positive action or positive discrimination can be a good reason for differential treatment – as long as it is proportionate. An example of positive action is shown in the following case illustration.

Case illustration: positive action

During the 1980s the European Court of Human Rights gave a ruling on a case taken against the British government in relation to the taxation system. The couple who took the case believed that it was wrong for married couples, where the husband was the only wage earner, to be taxed more than married couples in which the wife was the only wage earner. The British government argued that the extra tax allowance for women had been intended to encourage more married women to work. The government thought this allowance was necessary because in the past prejudice in the workplace had prevented married women from working. The tax break was therefore an incentive. The government also pointed out that only three per cent of tax payers were affected by the system – and that they intended to change the law to equalise the tax system. They believed the incentive was no longer necessary. The Court's ruling recognised that governments have to be able to strike a balance between its taxation policies and what it called 'other societal objectives' such as encouraging women to work. The Court said that the taxation policy 'has an objective and reasonable justification in the aim of providing positive discrimination in favour of married women who work.' They also found that the policy was proportionate in its application.

4   What would lessen the disproportionate impact?

5   If this alternative has been rejected, what are the reasons?

4.17   These questions tackle in more detail any of the alternatives to the policy that is proposed. The principle of proportionality is similar to the old saying 'don't take a sledgehammer to crack a nut'. Even if the reasons are good, and the differential treatment that you will put in place is justified, it may still be that there is a less disproportionate policy that could apply. Think about the group of people whose rights will be most affected. Is there another alternative that could achieve the policy aim, but have less impact on their rights?

4.18   If there is and it has already been rejected, write it down, and note next to it the reasons why this is so. At this stage there may be a clear alternative proposal that might have less impact on individuals' rights but still achieve the policy outcome. Your organisation may want to choose to pursue this instead.

4.19   When you have answered these questions, review your answers so far. If there are good reasons for what you intend to do, and the outcome of the policy is not too disproportionate in relation to these aims, move on. If on the other hand your reasons are thin and the impact of your policy looks as if it might be considerable, it may be sensible to seek legal advice before proceeding with the policy.

Communicating the decision

6   Is there a particular group of people that would find it difficult to find out about the way in which the policy or decision might impact on their rights? Who?

7   How can it be made clear to this group of people how their rights might be affected?

8   If the restriction on rights is a response to an individual's behaviour or conduct, how can this be communicated effectively to all likely to be affected?

4.20   This final section of the discrimination checklist covers the communication of the decision that has been made. One way of avoiding discrimination is to think about how people that will be affected by the decision will find out about it. Don't assume that everyone is the same, and can find out about the change in the same way, or that they will all need the same type of information to fully understand the consequences of a policy change. Some examples of this are shown in the case illustration that follows.

4.21 Will some groups of people find it more difficult than others to find out how their rights are affected? If they will, note down how the organisation intends to compensate for this. The importance and obligation of providing information to people about their rights has long been recognised in human rights law – there is more information about this in Part II of the *Human Rights Act Toolkit* and in section three of the checklist on page 28 above that deals with positive obligations.

4.22 Failing to see the consequences of not informing people about changes to the law – or not informing all those who will be affected – could be an unintended impact of the proposal, and could lead to indirect discrimination. Making this question explicit and addressing it early in the process will ensure that this is avoided.

Case illustrations: preventing discrimination in the provision of information

A housing project running supported accommodation for people with learning disabilities, and for people with mental health problems, has recently changed its guidelines on tenant behaviour to ensure that all tenants feel safe in their homes. The residents in one building – all of whom have learning disabilities – need to have information presented in an accessible way to ensure they understand the implications of policies. After consulting with residents, staff decide to run a special workshop to make sure that everyone really does understand the impact of their behaviour on their ability to keep their home and can discuss it together, rather than simply sending out a leaflet to all residents.

A housing department intends to run a campaign focusing on the council's new policy of assertive pursuit of rent arrears, leading to eviction if there is non-payment. Staff are concerned that in some areas of the city, the tenants won't understand the campaign – literacy levels are low, and English is usually a second or third language. They decide to run radio ads and produce posters in a local community language as well as English to make sure that all tenants know and understand the consequences of their actions.

CHAPTER 5

Worked case examples

Introduction

5.1   These case examples work through the checklist on a step by step basis to illustrate the type of issues and challenges that can be thrown up by the Human Rights Act framework, and ways in which they could be resolved. They are written in note form, as if by a manager or following a team discussion, and are intended to be illustrations. They should not be taken as legal advice.

Case example one: planning process

5.2   A local authority has received a planning application from a company that want to build an energy recovery and waste transfer station. The timing means this application will be considered under current planning law, ahead of any changes outlined in the 2007 Planning White Paper. This incinerator would receive rubbish from local residents and burn it to create energy. The incinerator would be built on a brownfield site on a main road, but it is reasonably close to a residential area with many restored Georgian houses, as well as an estate with a large Somali community and a school. Staff members need to consider the application, and develop a consultation process which takes into account the Human Rights Act, using the checklist format to shape their initial team discussion.

5.3   The worked case example illustrates the application of Human Rights Act principles to the day to day decision making process and the design of a consultation process. For the purpose of this example, the detail of planning law, and the impact of various environmental regulations, has been omitted.

Section one – the policy area or decision making process

1.1   What is the policy or process that is being developed?
Consultation process to ensure that the planning decision is robust and transparent – and enables public participation

1.2   Why is it needed and what is its purpose?
Application for transfer of use has been received: Council needs to consider and decide whether to grant the application. Purpose of the process is to ensure that all affected parties have the ability to feed in their views, and that Council can take account of these in the final decision.

Section two – identification of rights

2.1   *Make a note of any rights that could be affected by the policy or process, and identify whose rights are affected.*

- Article 6 rights – but dealt with at the court stage because opponents can apply for the decision to be reviewed through judicial review. However, we want to try and be in line with article 6 to stop this happening. Residents and the company concerned. [Need to do the mini checklist too.]
- Article 8 rights – people will argue that the incinerator affects their right to private and family life because it changes their quality of life. They will argue that the pollution – and for some of them maybe additional traffic – will have a negative impact on their quality of life. Residents – lots of them!
- Article 14 rights – will some residents argue that we are discriminating against them because of where they live? They have to link it to something else – probably article 8 or article 1, protocol 1. Residents again.
- Article 1, protocol 1 – people with gardens might argue that they don't want to use them any longer because of the emissions. Residents here too.
- Article 2, protocol 1 – one of my team thinks that a parent could argue the incinerator threatens their child's right to an education. I don't agree. But we might run it by the legal team.

Update: the legal team thinks the most relevant rights are article 6, article 8 and article 1, protocol 1. Article 14 and article 2, protocol 1 are not relevant.

2.2   *Look again at each of the rights identified in the answer to question 2.1. Will your policy or process impact on any of these rights? Does it protect them or interfere with them in a way that might restrict them? Give an answer for each right you have identified.*

We should make sure we protect article 6 rights which will probably deal with access to information as it relates to our situation. As for the rest – people will argue that we are interfering with them or restricting them in every case. We'll need to look at the main checklist, the mini checklist for article 6 and perhaps for article 14 too, though I'd like the lawyer to think about that one before we get started.

Section three – protection of rights

3.1   *The Human Rights Act may impose a positive obligation (or special duty) to protect some rights. Is there any way in which this could be relevant?*
Yes, in that article 8 is one of the rights that is of fundamental importance. So, we might have a positive obligation to protect it.

3.2   *If you have answered 'yes' to question 3.1, identify whose rights are affected*
Local residents – they can rely on their article 8 rights.

3.3   *Identify the action that might need to be taken to protect these rights*
This is really looking ahead. Looking at the four principles on page 31 above, it's not really about resources. However, if the company got permission to build the incinerator, I guess we'd have to make sure we kept an eye on the emissions via the Environment Agency to ensure that they weren't breaching any limits or upper levels – that would meet the duty to prevent breaches of rights. We'd obviously need to respond in some way if they were, otherwise someone might challenge us or the power company.

The one that is most relevant to us right now is the provision of information. If people's rights could be at risk, we'll need to provide information to help them decide what they want to do – even if that means they challenge us in court. Or some of them might decide to move house.

I suppose in relation to information provision, we might want to think now about how we will monitor emissions in the future. That means that we'll be able to show during the consultation how we plan to take steps to avoid a risk to residents' rights in the future.

3.4   *Who needs to know about this action and who will have the final responsibility to make sure that it happens?*
In terms of providing information for the consultation process, our team. Final responsibility: me.

In terms of the monitoring, I'll talk to environmental health.

Section four – restricting and balancing rights

4.1 *Think about the person whose rights could be restricted. How will they find out about the decision?*
We're not restricting it as such, more like impacting upon it. They will find out because we'll tell them and invite them to participate in a consultation process.

4.2 *Identify the legitimate aim that you are trying to meet.*
If they agree the decision they'll argue the protection of the economy: we save on sending waste to landfill, and we recycle to produce energy as will other local boroughs. Plus it will create jobs.

4.3 *Are you restricting one person's rights to protect the rights of another individual? If so, explain whose right will be restricted and whose is protected, and why this is necessary.*
No, not really.

4.4 *Is there another way that to achieve the aim identified in question 4.2? If there is, note it.*
Not relevant – looking back at the checklist examples, it's not as if we're dealing with different people's rights, like the sex offender example. We'd have to consider the planning application anyway – it's the law.

4.5 *What is the reason for not adopting the approach identified in the answer to question 4.4?*
Not relevant.

4.6 *Think about the diversity of clients, staff and service users that your organisation works with. Would the answer to question 2.2 be different if considered from another perspective?*
We'll need to check this actually. One of my colleagues thinks that the estate closest to the incinerator has a big Somali community. That has all kinds of implications for the consultation process – and it could look bad if we don't get it right. It also means we need to take article 14 more seriously than I'd thought: it certainly could be used.

Update: the legal team agrees and revises its advice. The team need to think about article 14 in relation to this planning application as it could be linked to article 8 to mount a subsequent legal challenge.

Section five – organisational process

5.1   *Who has been consulted about this policy or procedure?*
This is internal – so we'll pull in colleagues from all the usual teams, including communications, and the legal side.

5.2   *Who must agree to the policy or procedure before it can be finalised?*
Councillors will need to sign off the consultation process, and of course they will agree the final decision.

5.3   *How will people get the training and information they need to ensure that the policy or procedure works?*
Front line staff at the one-stop-shop will need to have details about the consultation process. That's about it: there are no big training issues.

Mini checklist – the right to a fair trial

1   *Does the policy or decision impact on someone's civil rights – and if so, what are these?*
Yes: it's pretty clear that planning is a civil rights issue. We've already had guidance on that.

2   *What kind of appeal process exists if someone disagrees with the decision?*
Planning inspectors, and the High Court for the company applying. For residents' groups, judicial review: it's a frequently used process. It challenges our decision in court.

3   *Does the decision making process allow the person access to a court to challenge the decision at some stage during the process?*
Yes – see above.

4   *Does the individual whose rights are affected have the ability to participate in the decision making process at some stage? If not, are the reasons for this likely to be considered necessary under the Human Rights Act?*
Yes, we'll make sure they do. They can put in submissions, give evidence at the public meeting, and lobby their local councillor – all sorts. They can be present when the decision is made because it will be taken in public. All the documents we receive will be made public where we can, and that will ensure people have all the information they need. We'll also try and make the consultation process run over a reasonable

time. Of course they can go to court anyway which will guarantee their article 6 rights.

5 *Is the person whose rights are affected provided with the reasons for the decision when it is made? If not, can the decision making process be amended so that this is possible?*
Since the Human Rights Act came into force we've been giving more reasons in any case, and we always have had to give reasons if we say no. It's if we say yes that's the thing. With something like this we'll certainly need to. I'll speak to people about this.

6 *Is there a review process that can scrutinise the decision? If so, is the tribunal or review panel independent, and operating within the relevant human rights principles?*
It goes to the Planning Inspector, who isn't independent, but then to the courts, and they are. We're OK here.

Article 6 and public consultation

7 *Does the consultation process take account of the relevant article 6 principles?*
Yes, we're building them in. We'll have a public meeting to enable participation from the residents' groups, and from the local environmental group that works in the borough. They can also make submissions if they want to do so. We'll make the documents public at the Town Hall, and we'll hold the final decision making meeting in public, and if we can, we'll put a lot of the documents on the internet too. I'm going to suggest that we get an independent report into the impact of the incinerator. That would be a really good way to demonstrate that we're looking at the decision seriously, and would probably reassure councillors that they would have good information to consider.

8 *Does the process range as widely as possible amongst a cross-section of people that might be affected by the decision?*
Yes, and we're going to make a real effort to involve the Somali community: we've got someone translating leaflets already, and we'll have interpreters at the public meeting. We might hold a separate meeting for that community depending on the advice we get from local people.

9   *Does the consultation process give people the opportunity to understand the reasons for the decision that is taken at the end of the process?*
       Yes, we'll make sure it does – see 5 above. The particular things to be careful of are if councillors make a decision that isn't in line with officers' recommendations. That's when we will certainly need to explain it – whichever way they decide.

Mini checklist – discrimination

1   *Could the decision constitute differential treatment?*
       If we decided to do a consultation process that didn't take account of the community's particular needs, I think it could, yes. However, not the planning decision itself, that doesn't vary.

2   *If there is differential treatment, is it justified? If yes, explain this.*
       No. Of course some people here would like it if we did a nice easy consultation process, and we need to avoid that. It needs not to be administratively convenient.

3   *If there is differential treatment, is the policy proportionate to the outcome that it will produce? Explain how this is so.*
       We're going to try and make sure this doesn't happen.

4   *What would lessen the disproportionate impact?*
       Running a good process.

5   *If this alternative has been rejected, what are the reasons?*
       The team have gone for it and the budget is there, so we're OK on this one.

6   *Is there a particular group of people that would find it difficult to find out about the way in which the policy or decision might impact on their rights? Who?*
       Yes, the local Somali community.

7   *How can it be made clear to this group of people how their rights might be affected?*
       Interpreters and information provided in a way that this community can understand – the right language, the right format. Taking account of the fact that many people are wary of evening meetings – there's a fear factor on that estate unfortunately. Encouraging participation – many of the

residents were originally refugees, so will people feel that they really can speak up? We need to make sure they do. We'll need to tell them not just about the incinerator but about the whole process that we're running. Not sure that all of this can be translated, but we'll do what we can.

8   *If the restriction on rights is a response to an individual's behaviour or conduct, how can this be communicated effectively to all likely to be affected?*
Doesn't apply in this case.

Case example two: re-housing a sex offender

5.4   A local authority receives a request from the family of a sex offender, previously a local resident. He is to be released from prison to return to his family – his wife and children. The family are concerned that they will not be safe if he returns to live in their existing home. They want to be re-housed. The worked case example illustrates the application of Human Rights Act principles to the day to day decision making process, particularly in relation to balancing rights. For the purpose of this example, detailed housing law has been omitted.

Section one – the policy area or decision making process

1.1   *What is the decision, policy or process that is being developed?*
Decision making process that takes account of the Human Rights Act in the re-housing of a sex offender and his family.

1.2   *Why is it needed and what is its purpose?*
A risk management situation – we need this decision to take account of local children's rights and any obligations we may have, as well as the rights of the family.

Section two – identification of rights

2.1   *Make a note of any rights that could be affected, and identify whose rights they are.*

- Article 2 and 3 rights – the ex-offender's. If the local community hear he's out, he could potentially be at risk, as could his family.

- Article 3 rights – local kids, to stop the abuse happening again, depending on severity it could constitute inhuman or degrading treatment. This is crucially important for us.
- Article 6 rights – the family because if they don't like our decision they will want to appeal against it.
- Article 8 rights – the ex-offender's and his family presumably. His family have the right to respect for their home and family life, and he probably does too.
- Article 8 rights – the ex-offender has the right to privacy – we shouldn't tell the world what he's done though obviously he's on the sex offenders register: that's an acceptable limitation and a result of his crime. We're not sure if he has a probation officer because the circumstances of his release aren't yet clear so we need to find out.
- Article 8 rights – local kids again – probably depends what they would be at risk from, but abuse is obviously a violation of bodily integrity. So if it wasn't article 3 it would fit here.
- Article 10 rights – local parents may argue this. The local community know he's coming out and they will want to know where he's going. They will argue they have a right to know to protect their children.
- Article 14 – ex-offender and family: can we treat them any differently from another resident? Would that be discrimination?

2.2   *Look again at each of the rights identified in the answer to question 2.1. Will the decision, policy or process impact on any of these rights? Does it protect them or interfere with them in a way that might restrict them? Give an answer for each right identified.*
The trigger for the move is his article 2 rights, which we have to protect – we can't allow him to return to a situation where we know he could be at that much risk. If we agree to move him, the most important thing is the rights of local children – they need to be safe, so that's protecting their article 3 and 8 rights. Alternatively we could decide that it is reasonable to allow the family to continue to live where they are, and monitor the threat. At the moment, that doesn't look like an option. There are already leaflets and petitions circulating.

If he was returning to his old home, the rights of local children would still be most important. We'd have to move him into an alternative property in any case because right now they live on an estate near a school and the kids' rights would be at risk then.

Then we would need to show respect for the offender's family: they have rights under article 8, as does he, but both of those are secondary to the children's rights. Because they need to move, and because of where we will put them, their home won't be as nice as it is now: that will arguably interfere with their rights.

We'll need to safeguard as much as we can of the ex-offender's article 8 rights to privacy – and obviously protect his right to life, that's article 2.

We will be restricting the local parent's rights under article 10 – we can show that we have already balanced different rights against each other.

We are putting the children's article 8 rights first by keeping his location out of the public domain.

Section three – protection of rights

3.1   *The Human Rights Act may impose a positive obligation (or special duty) to protect some rights. Is there any way in which this could be relevant?*
Yes, if the article 3 and 8 rights apply to local children we could have a positive obligation under these rights because they are both of such fundamental importance. And article 2 rights give us a positive obligation to protect both the ex-offender and his family from any risk to their lives.

3.2   *If you have answered 'yes' to question 3.1, identify whose rights are affected.*
The local children – they need to be protected from his actions if he should offend again. So we will have to take that into account when we decide where to re-house him.

The ex-offender and his family – their lives could be at risk – that's article 2, and that's why we need to move him in the first place.

3.3   *Identify the action that might need to be taken to protect these rights.*
Criminal justice agencies will already know: police and probation may have a monitoring programme in place. We

will notify social services so that they can update the sex offenders register, and liaise with the police.

There are two options for re-housing. The first estate where we have property is not so nice, but it has empty flats. It's all council rented, so at least we will have good records and control – we will know whether there are other families living there. We can't put him somewhere where there is a family with kids, particularly not if the family is vulnerable. The second area is nicer, but has more of a mix of council and private rented, so we don't hold enough information on whether or not there are families around. Also the first place is further away from any schools.

In relation to protection for the children's article 3 and 8 rights, if we tell residents where the guy is he may well disappear. That means the contact with the police and probation will be lost. Kids will be even more at risk if there is no monitoring. So that means restricting parents' right to know, in order to safeguard the obligation we have to protect local children.

3.4   *Who needs to know about this action and who has the final responsibility to make sure that it happens?*
My team: to notify social services, get them to talk to his probation contact, and we can do the same. Also my team should inform the local housing office and the police.

Section four – balancing rights

4.1   *Think about the person whose rights could be restricted. How will they find out about the decision?*
The local residents won't find out: we need to protect the kids' rights so we won't be telling everyone where he is.

The family won't like the property we're planning to allocate as much as where they are now, but they will obviously find out because we'll tell them.

4.2   *Identify the legitimate aim that you are trying to meet.*
Lots: public safety in relation to the children's rights, the prevention of crime in case he offends again and the protection of the rights and freedoms of others in relation to the children's rights. All of these apply to why we need to move them to another less attractive home.

4.3 *Are you restricting one person's rights to protect the rights of another individual? If so, explain whose right will be restricted, whose is protected, and why this is necessary.*
This is strong ground. We need to protect the rights of local children – including their right to be free from degrading treatment – article 3. We need to protect his right to life and rights under article 3. So we are restricting the rights of the offender and his family by moving them to a different home. It's necessary because without doing so he will almost certainly have his life threatened. But then, if we do move him, we absolutely must have as our first priority the rights of local children.

However, because we are providing the family with a new home, we are not taking that much away from their article 8 rights: very little at all in fact. They still have a home.

4.4 *Is there another way to achieve the aim identified in question 4.2? If there is, note it.*
He could stay in the family home and we could monitor the risk to him and his family.

4.5 *What is the reason for not adopting the approach identified in the answer to question 4.4?*
The risk at the moment appears to be too great and puts his own child at risk.

4.6 *Think about the diversity of clients, staff and service users that your organisation works with. Would the answer to question 2.2 be different if considered from another perspective? How?*
No.

Section five – organisational process

5.1 *Who has been consulted about this policy or procedure?*
He should be registered with social services and the police should be aware of his address as well as the local MAPPA team. Things like this have a habit of becoming public and we should tell the communications team, or think about what we want to say if it does become public. We need to show that we have used the Human Rights Act to put the rights of local children first in this re-housing decision.

5.2   *Who must agree to the policy or procedure before it can be finalised?*
My boss.

5.3   *How will people get the training and information they need to ensure that the policy or procedure works?*
Social services need to understand the implication of the positive obligation we have, as does the local housing officer. It might be worth seeing if we can get people together to talk this through and liaise with any MAPPA or probation contact.

Mini checklist – the right to a fair trial

1   *Does the policy or decision impact on someone's civil rights – and if so, what are these?*
Could do – it's re-housing.

2   *What kind of appeal process exists if someone disagrees with the decision?*
There is no internal appeal process because the family isn't homeless. We might need to look at this.

3   *Does the decision making process allow the person access to a court to challenge the decision at some stage during the process?*
Yes, because the family can go to court and challenge our decision on the grounds that the lack of appeal process is a violation of their human rights under article 6. I don't think they will, but they could. So that's a guarantee.

4   *Does the individual whose rights are affected have the ability to participate in the decision making process at some stage? If not, are the reasons for this likely to be considered necessary under the Human Rights Act?*
No – you only get one housing offer in our borough because of the shortage of properties. So the only chance they get is if they challenge the lack of an appeal process in court.

5   *Is the person whose rights are affected provided with the reasons for the decision when it is made? If not, can the decision making process be amended so that this is possible?*
We will tell the family where we have allocated and why. Then if they challenge it in court, they obviously will be given reasons for the decision by the judge.

6   *Is there a review process that can scrutinise the decision? If so, is the tribunal or review panel independent, and operating within the relevant human rights principles?*
No. Perhaps we should look at this and find out what others do to have some sort of independent scrutiny. But that is a longer term decision.

Mini checklist – discrimination

1   *Could the decision constitute differential treatment?*
Perhaps they would argue that we are discriminating because we're asking them to move somewhere less pleasant and that we're doing so because he's an ex-offender. I suppose it's possible.

2   *If there is differential treatment, is it justified? If yes, explain this.*
If they argue that they are being discriminated against because of his offending behaviour, I'd say we have a very strong case – we're not only protecting local children's rights but we're protecting his own rights!

3   *If there is differential treatment, is the policy proportionate to the outcome that it will produce? Explain how this is so.*
Yes, we're giving them a new home, so the impact is minimal. It's not as if we are taking away their home and not providing them with an alternative.

4   *What would lessen the disproportionate impact?*
Placing them in a slightly nicer area, similar to where they are now.

5   *If this alternative has been rejected, what are the reasons?*
There are too many unknowns; we don't have enough information about how many families live there because much of the accommodation is private, and it's closer to a school. It's not appropriate to move a sex offender into that situation – we'd be risking falling short of the positive obligation that we have to protect the children's rights.

6   *Is there a particular group of people that would find it difficult to find out about the way in which the policy or decision might impact on their rights? Who?*
No.

7   *How can it be made clear to this group of people how their rights might be affected?*
Doesn't apply.

8   *If the restriction on rights is a response to an individual's behaviour or conduct, how can this be communicated effectively to all likely to be affected?*
We can communicate it to him – that's quite straightforward. We can explain to him the reasons why we need to allocate him and his family onto the estate with fewer families: it's a response to his offending behaviour, and our need to keep local children safe.

CHAPTER 6

The checklist questions

The main checklist

Section one – the policy area or decision making process

1.1   What is the decision, policy or process that is being developed?

1.2   Why is it needed and what is its purpose?

Section two – identification of rights

2.1   Make a note of any rights that could be affected, and identify whose rights they are.

2.2   Look again at each of the rights identified in the answer to question 2.1. Will the decision, policy or process impact on any of these rights? Does it protect them or interfere with them in a way that might restrict them? Give an answer for each right identified.

Section three – protection of rights

3.1   The Human Rights Act may impose a positive obligation (or special duty) to protect some rights. Is there any way in which this could be relevant?

3.2   If you have answered 'yes' to question 3.1, identify whose rights are affected.

3.3   Identify the action that might need to be taken to protect these rights.

3.4   Who needs to know about this action and who has the final responsibility to make sure that it happens?

Section four – balancing rights

4.1   Think about the person whose rights could be restricted. How will they find out about the decision?

4.2   Identify the legitimate aim that you are trying to meet.

4.3   Are you restricting one person's rights to protect the rights of another individual? If so, explain whose right will be restricted, whose is protected, and why this is necessary.

4.4 Is there another way to achieve the aim identified in question 4.2? If there is, note it.

4.5 What is the reason for not adopting the approach identified in the answer to question 4.4?

4.6 Think about the diversity of clients, staff and service users that your organisation works with. Would the answer to question 2.2 be different if considered from another perspective? How?

Section five – organisational process

5.1 Who has been consulted about this policy or procedure?

5.2 Who must agree to the policy or procedure before it can be finalised?

5.3 How will people get the training and information they need to ensure that the policy or procedure works?

Mini checklist: the right to a fair trial

1 Does the policy or decision impact on someone's civil rights – and if so, what are these?

2 What kind of appeal process exists if someone disagrees with the decision?

3 Does the decision making process allow the person access to a court to challenge the decision at some stage during the process?

4 Does the individual whose rights are affected have the ability to participate in the decision making process at some stage? If not, are the reasons for this likely to be considered necessary under the Human Rights Act?

5 Is the person whose rights are affected provided with the reasons for the decision when it is made? If not, can the decision making process be amended so that this is possible?

6 Is there a review process that can scrutinise the decision? If so, is the tribunal or review panel independent, and operating within the relevant human rights principles?

Article 6 and public consultation

7   Does the consultation process take account of the relevant article 6 principles?

8   Does the process range as widely as possible amongst a cross-section of people that might be affected by the decision?

9   Does the consultation process give people the opportunity to understand the reasons for the decision that is taken at the end of the process?

Mini checklist: discrimination

1   Could the decision constitute differential treatment?

2   If there is differential treatment, is it justified? If yes, explain this.

3   If there is differential treatment, is the policy proportionate to the outcome that it will produce? Explain how this is so.

4   What would lessen the disproportionate impact?

5   If this alternative has been rejected, what are the reasons?

6   Is there a particular group of people that would find it difficult to find out about the way in which the policy or decision might impact on their rights? Who?

7   How can it be made clear to this group of people how their rights might be affected?

8   If the restriction on rights is a response to an individual's behaviour or conduct, how can this be communicated effectively to all likely to be affected?

PART II

The Law

The significance of the Human Rights Act 1998

Introduction

7.1   This chapter will provide background information to help you understand the importance of the Human Rights Act 1998, possibly the most far-reaching piece of legislation ever to have been passed by Parliament. The Act has a pervasive effect over all UK law. It imposes duties on public sector organisations as well as on those charities and private bodies carrying out public functions.[1] One of the longer-term aims of the Human Rights Act is to develop a culture of rights-based thinking within society that guarantees minimum standards in order to ensure respect for the fundamental rights and freedoms of every person.

7.2   The rights contained in the Human Rights Act are neither new nor experimental. The Act incorporates provisions contained in the Convention for the Protection of Human Rights and Fundamental Freedoms 1950, more commonly known as the European Convention on Human Rights, into UK law. Many of these rights are recognised in the constitutions of a number of countries throughout the world.

7.3   This chapter will consider why the Human Rights Act is necessary, before examining the importance of the European Convention on Human Rights, and the implications of its incorporation into UK law. Finally, this chapter will list the other international human rights treaties signed by the United Kingdom, and outline their relevance to UK law.

The need for the Human Rights Act 1998

7.4   The Human Rights Act is not the first legal document to strike at the heart of the set of fundamental principles according to which this country is structured and governed; our Constitution. The Magna Carta and the 1689 Bill of Rights were both momentous documents in our constitutional history. The Magna Carta was primarily concerned with redistributing power between the King and his nobles, while the 1689 Bill of Rights focused on changing the structure of power from the divine right of the monarch towards the idea of a sovereign Parliament. In contrast, the Human Rights Act

---

1   See chapter 11 at paras 11.16 – 11.27.

1998 is not so much concerned with the redistribution of power to a more representative group, as with protecting the fundamental rights of all individuals within the UK.

7.5　　Prior to the passing of the Human Rights Act, Parliament held the dominant Constitutional role in protecting the rights and freedoms of those living in the UK. The Victorian constitutional authority, AV Dicey, stated that a sovereign Parliament protected the fundamental freedoms of citizens by allowing them to do whatever they wanted unless their action was contrary to the laws of the land or impaired the legal rights of others. The question of where to draw this legal line was one for Parliament to decide. However, Dicey believed that two checks could be relied upon to prevent the excessive use of parliament's authority to the detriment of civil liberties. The first was the commitment of Members of Parliament to highlight and oppose any infringements to fundamental rights during parliamentary debate. The second was the force of public opinion, since those who pass laws are reliant on the support of the public for their legitimacy. However, these two checks are not always sufficient to protect civil liberties, especially those of minority or vulnerable groups.

7.6　　The limitations of these checks were most graphically highlighted in Germany towards the middle of the twentieth century with the legislation passed by Adolf Hitler's democratically elected National Socialist Party. For example, Hitler used the burning down of the German Parliament, the Reichstag, (an act that was, in fact, carried out by the Nazis) to justify legislation that was 'required for the protection of the people and the state'. Accordingly, when introducing the 1933 Enabling Acts, he stated that:

> Restrictions on personal liberty, on the right of free expression and opinion, including freedom of the press, on the right of assembly and associations; and violations of the privacy of postal, telegraphic, and telephonic communications and warrants for house searches, orders for confiscations as well as restrictions on property are also permissible beyond the legal limits otherwise prescribed.

7.7　　Laws of this type opened the way for the atrocities which were perpetrated against large numbers of minority groups in Germany and shocked the conscience of the world.

The importance of the European Convention on Human Rights

7.8   Events in Europe, which showed the level of barbarity that could be carried out against one's own people, prompted the international community at the end of the Second World War to formulate a set of fundamental values belonging to all individuals. The result was the Universal Declaration of Human Rights adopted by the General Assembly of the United Nations in 1948. In Europe, the sensitivity of states to the events that had taken place resulted in the founding of the Council of Europe in 1949.[2] Its aim was to create a Europe that was based on common principles of respect and understanding.

7.9   The first task for the countries that joined the Council of Europe was to draft a legally binding treaty protecting the fundamental rights of people in member countries. The European Convention on Human Rights was completed in November 1950. The UK was the first country to sign the treaty in 1951. By signing up to an international human rights treaty, a country agrees to act in accordance with the provisions of that treaty.[3]

7.10   As well as including the articles protecting human rights, the European Convention also contains provisions about the procedures and workings of the European Court of Human Rights, which is the principal body designed to oversee the implementation of the Convention. Even before the drafting was completed in 1950, it was recognised that the Convention did not cover the full list of civil and political rights.[4] Consequently, there have, so far, been fourteen additional protocols. Each protocol needs to be signed by a country in order to be binding upon it. Six of the protocols contain additional rights to those set out in the 1950 Convention. The UK has signed two: the first and the sixth optional protocols.[5] Those protocols that do not establish additional rights are concerned with procedural issues and, most importantly, the running of the Court system.

2   This is a completely separate organisation from the European Community established under the Treaty of Rome in 1957, which is concerned with economic integration in Europe. However, it should be noted that the Charter of Fundamental Rights of the European Union was drafted in 2000.

3   There are, as at September 2007, 47 European countries that are a party to the European Convention.

4   The European Convention does not include economic, social and cultural rights. See para 7.28 below.

5   These are set out in chapter 8 at paras 8.131– 8.146.

7.11   The European Convention contains a complaints mechanism which allows individuals in a country which has signed up to the Convention to bring their case before a specially established tribunal, the European Court of Human Rights, which is based in Strasbourg.[6] An individual may only bring a complaint to the European Court if they believe that their domestic courts have failed to recognise or remedy the right which is claimed to have been violated.

7.12   The complaints mechanism was particularly important prior to the passing of the Human Rights Act. While treaties are legally binding on those states that sign up to them, in a number of countries, such as the UK, these treaty provisions can only be claimed by individuals before their own courts if they have been adopted into domestic law through an Act of Parliament.[7]

7.13   Before the Human Rights Act was passed, the decisions of the European Court played a particularly important role in the protection of human rights in the UK. The UK's record before the European Court was far from satisfactory. A number of violations have been found covering every Convention right. A UK citizen who believed a Convention right had been violated would have to go through the time and expense of exhausting their domestic legal remedies before being able to bring a complaint before the European Court. If the Strasbourg Court found that the UK authorities had failed to protect the Convention rights of the individual, it would find a violation. The UK government would then be expected, in accordance with its international law obligations, to change its laws or procedures to ensure that it was acting compatibly with the Convention. The decisions of the European Court have been responsible for many changes to UK law.[8]

7.14   It should be noted that the fact that the UK courts can now apply the Convention when reaching their decisions does not mean that those in the UK have no more use for the Strasbourg tribunal. Cases

---

6   This is not to be confused with the European Court of Justice which is concerned with European Community issues and sits in Luxembourg.

7   The courts could in rare situations apply these human rights provisions where the law was ambiguous or uncertain. This is because the UK courts adopted the approach that governments would not intend to apply laws to a standard which was below their international obligations. See, for example, *R v Secretary for the Home Department ex p Brind* [1991] 1 AC 969.

8   For example, the Mental Health Act 1983 was introduced as a direct result of a violation found in *X v United Kingdom* (1982) 4 EHRR 188.

may still be brought if an individual believes that the domestic courts have not recognised or remedied a Convention breach.

The implications of incorporating the European Convention on Human Rights into UK law

7.15   The support for the introduction of legislation adopting the provisions of the European Convention into UK law began to gain momentum over the final third of the twentieth century. The need for the Convention to be incorporated into UK law became increasingly apparent as the decisions in Strasbourg revealed that a wide range of UK laws did not meet the minimum requirements set down by the European Convention. In addition, the process for taking a case to the European Court was both slow and costly, since a person would first have to try and seek a remedy before the UK courts or tribunals.

7.16   Support for human rights legislation did not divide itself along party lines. This is because human rights are not the invention or property of any political party. Support and opposition for the adoption of the European Convention into UK law could be found among all political parties. There were three main issues that dominated the debate as to whether the Convention should be incorporated into UK law.

The threat to the sovereignty of parliament

7.17   It was argued that the introduction of human rights legislation would weaken our system of parliamentary sovereignty because it would place Parliament under a duty to act in accordance with rights and principles established under the European Convention. However, the political reality was that the ever-increasing power and reach of Parliament, and more particularly, central government, had resulted in its increasing detachment from the electorate. In the early 1990s, The Rt Hon John Smith MP, then leader of the Labour Party, who was the first leader of a major political party to endorse the idea of incorporation, argued that constitutional reform was needed in order to put people at the centre of the democratic process. He stated that he wanted:

A deal that gives people new powers and a stronger voice in the affairs of the nation ... I want to see a fundamental shift in the balance of power between citizen and the state – a shift away from an overpowering state to a citizen's democracy where people have rights and powers and where they are served by accountable and responsible government.[9]

The fear of 'alien values' being adopted into the UK

7.18　From the moment that the adoption of the European Convention into UK law was first mooted, there was opposition, particularly from senior judges, that it would result in the introduction of alien principles that would conflict with the culture that had developed in the UK. This opposition was seemingly oblivious to the instrumental role that the UK had played in the drafting of the Convention.

7.19　Many of the judges feared that high-sounding Convention rights would be used by undeserving, disgruntled or subversive individuals seeking to undermine or embarrass the orderly system under which the country was run. However, the judgments coming from the European Court helped to win over many of the sceptics. Their decisions showed that the Court was not trying to establish a rigid European legal code based on alien concepts, but to ensure that the legal code of each country secured minimum standards of human rights. It also became clear that the Court was not concerned with protecting individual rights to the detriment of the community. Instead, the decisions of the European Court highlighted the overriding importance which it attached to the object and purpose of the Convention, namely the protection of not only individual rights, but the ideas and values that lay at the heart of a democratic society.[10] By the time the government introduced their White Paper on the Human Rights Bill, just about all the senior members of the judiciary were in support, including some who had previously been vehemently opposed.

The politicisation of the courts

7.20　There was particular concern that the passing of the Human Rights Act would transfer power away from a democratically elected parliament to an unelected and unaccountable judiciary that would

9　M Zander, *A Bill of Rights?* (4th edn, Sweet & Maxwell, 1997) at p33.
10　See chapter 10 at para 10.4.

be able to strike down legislation and policy which, they believed contravened the Convention. A related fear was that this would result in the courts becoming more politicised. As then Prime Minister, Tony Blair emphasised the positive consequences of allowing the UK courts to determine cases involving Convention rights. He remarked that:

> Some have said that the system takes power away from Parliament and places it in the hands of judges. In reality, since we are already signatories to the Convention it means allowing British judges rather than European judges to pass judgment.[11]

7.21   However, this did not answer concerns about the effect of incorporation on the role and relationship of Parliament and the judiciary. This approach, which the government adopted to strike a balance between Parliament and the judiciary, only became known when the Human Rights Bill was introduced.[12] The role that is to be taken by the courts was considered in a case decided by the House of Lords. It concerned the indefinite detention of foreign nationals living in the UK who were suspected of involvement in terrorism. In the judgment, which ruled that indefinite detention was a breach of the European Convention on Human Rights, Lord Bingham stated:

> I do not in particular accept the distinction which the [Attorney General] drew between democratic institutions and the Court. It is of course true that the judges in this country are not elected and are not answerable to Parliament. It is of course true ... that Parliament, the executive, and the courts have different functions. But the function of independent judges charged to interpret and apply the law is universally recognised as a cardinal feature of the modern democratic state, a cornerstone of the rule of law itself. The Attorney General is fully entitled to insist on the proper limits of judicial authority, but he is wrong to stigmatise judicial decision-making as in some way undemocratic. It is particularly inappropriate in a case such as the present in which Parliament has expressly legislated in section 6 of the 1998 Act to render unlawful any act of a public authority, including a court, incompatible with a Convention right, has required courts (in section 2) to take account of relevant Strasbourg jurisprudence, has (in section 3) required courts, so far as possible, to give effect to Convention rights and has conferred a specific right of appeal on derogation issues ... The Human Rights Act gives the courts a very specific, wholly democratic, mandate...[13]

---

11   M Zander, *A Bill of Rights?* (4th edn, Sweet & Maxwell, 1997) at p38.

12   See chapter 11 at paras 11.5 – 11.12.

13   *A v Secretary of State for the Home Department* [2005] 2 WLR 87 at para 42.

7.22 In assessing the effectiveness of the Human Rights Act since it has come into force it is important not just to consider the impact of cases brought before the Courts. The awareness of the Act must stretch beyond lawyers to individuals and, importantly, to public authorities, if the UK is to develop a culture of respect for human rights within society. The need for greater awareness was highlighted in a study by the Audit Commission, which concluded that, 'In many local authorities the Act has not left the desk of the lawyers.'[14]

7.23 In addition to awareness-raising by NGOs, public bodies have a role to play in promoting and raising awareness of human rights issues within the UK. The Joint Committee on Human Rights, which consists of twelve members appointed from both the House of Commons and the House of Lords, scrutinises bills in order to test whether they comply with human rights obligations. The Joint Committee has also conducted a wide-range of inquiries into important human rights themes (such as deaths in custody, the human rights of people with learning difficulties and the role of economic and social rights in UK law). In conducting these inquiries it has taken evidence from a wider range of bodies.

7.24 On 1 October 2007, a new statutory body was created: the Equality and Human Rights Commission (EHRC). This body takes on the responsibilities of the previous single commissions (the Commission for Racial Equality, the Disability Rights Commission and the Equal Opportunities Commission) together with a broader equality agenda and will also act as a champion for human rights. Its mandate requires it to promote human rights culture, particularly ensuring that higher standards of dignity and respect are applied to vulnerable groups.

7.25 The role of Government appointed Chief Inspectors has also assisted in raising awareness of human rights concerns in the wider community. Reports from the Chief Inspector of Prisons were instrumental in identifying human rights breaches in young offender institutions.[15] The different chief inspectors have also joined to provide comprehensive reports on the arrangements to safeguard children.[16] The appointment of a Children's

---

14 Audit Commission 2003, 'Human Rights: Improving public service delivery'.

15 See *R v Secretary of State for the Home Department ex p The Howard League for Penal Reform* [2003] 1 FLR 484.

16 See, for example, the second joint Chief Inspector's Report on Arrangements to Safeguard Children. 'Safeguarding Children', July 2005.

Commissioner for England became a reality following the tragic institutional failings uncovered in the *Victoria Climbié* Inquiry.[17]

Other international human rights law treaties signed by the UK

7.26   The European Convention on Human Rights is not the only international human rights treaty that the UK has signed.

The main international human rights treaties signed by the UK include:

- the International Covenant on Civil and Political Rights 1966;
- the International Covenant on Economic, Social and Cultural Rights 1966;
- the Genocide Convention 1948;
- the Convention Against Torture, and Other Cruel, Inhuman and Degrading Treatment or Punishment 1984;
- the International Convention on the Elimination of All Forms of Racial Discrimination 1966;
- the Convention on the Elimination of All Forms of Discrimination Against Women 1979; and
- the Convention on the Rights of the Child 1989.

There are also a number of International Labour Organisation Conventions.

7.27   Before the Human Rights Act, only the Genocide Convention had been fully incorporated into UK law through the passing of the Genocide Act 1969. The Convention Against Torture, and Other Cruel, Inhuman or Degrading Treatment or Punishment was partially adopted under section 134 of the Criminal Justice Act 1988, and was a crucial factor in the House of Lords decision that it was lawful to extradite Augusto Pinochet to Spain.

---

17   The Office of the Children's Commissioner in England was established in the Children Act 2004 (Wales had already appointed a Children's Commissioner).

7.28   The European Convention is concerned with the protection of what are termed 'civil and political rights' as opposed to what are known as 'economic, social and cultural rights.' Economic, social and cultural rights which include the right to the highest attainable standard of health care and the right to social welfare services, have considerable resource implications. As a result, the obligation on governments has been to protect these rights to the maximum of their available resources. In view of the resource considerations, it was traditionally believed that it was not appropriate to make claims for economic, social and cultural rights before the courts. However, the case law of a number of other national courts, such as South Africa and India, has shown that there are elements to these rights that can be determined by the judiciary. There are now calls to incorporate provisions contained in the International Covenant on Economic, Social and Cultural Rights into UK law, which would be of assistance to the most vulnerable members of society who are often at greatest risk of social exclusion. The Joint Committee on Human Rights carried out a report on economic, social and cultural rights and concluded that greater attention needs to be given to the way in which the UK complies with the Covenant and put forward recommendations in an attempt to ensure that the rights contained in the Covenant are progressively realised in policy and legislation.[18]

7.29   Those international treaties, which the UK has signed up to but not incorporated, may still be relevant in circumstances where the law is ambiguous or uncertain.[19] They also have greater potential for relevance as a result of the adoption of the European Convention. Where a Convention right is affected, an unincorporated treaty, and especially one that concentrates on the rights of a particular social group, may help to establish or clarify the extent of the obligation owed by a public authority. This is because more recent and specific treaties often indicate how a human right standard has evolved or developed in that area.[20]

18 Joint Committee on Human Rights, *The International Covenant on Economic, Social and Cultural Rights* (Twenty-First Report, 2 November 2004).

19 See note 7 above.

20 For a consideration of evolving and developing rights see chapter 10 at para 10.10.

Case illustration

A mother contested the decision of the prison authorities to rigidly follow a policy which stated that a baby must be removed from the mother after they had spent the first eighteen months in prison together. She claimed that it violated their right to private and family life under article 8 of the European Convention since there was no other family to take the child. It was claimed that baby should not have to go through the upheaval of being placed in foster care for a short time before the mother was released. When considering whether the separation was justifiable, the Court of Appeal considered relevant provisions found in the United Nations Convention on the Rights of the Child 1989 to ensure that they were consistent with the case law on article 8 of the European Convention.[21]

---

21   *R v Secretary of State for the Home Department ex p P & Q* [2001] 1 WLR 2002.

CHAPTER 8

A breakdown of the Convention rights

Introduction

8.1 This chapter will analyse every substantive right contained in the European Convention and its protocols that have been incorporated into UK law through Schedule 1 of the Human Rights Act 1998. The scope of each right is not identical. The level of protection depends on the extent of the rights and duties that make up each Convention article.

8.2 A detailed analysis of the different types of rights and duties that are contained in the Convention articles and the principles which underpin them is to be found in chapters 9 and 10.

8.3 From time to time, a legal case name will be provided in the footnotes like this: *McCann v UK* (1995) 21 EHRR 97. Lawyers who want to know more about the case law may find these case references useful. However, the rights can also be understood without reference to the detailed point of law.[1]

Article 2 – right to life

(1) *Everyone's right to life shall be protected by law. No one shall be deprived of his life intentionally save in the execution of a sentence of a court following his conviction of a crime for which this penalty is provided by law.*

(2) *Deprivation of life shall not be regarded as inflicted in contravention of this article when it results from the use of force which is no more than absolutely necessary:*

   (a) *in defence of any person from unlawful violence;*
   (b) *in order to effect a lawful arrest or to prevent the escape of a person lawfully detained;*
   (c) *in action lawfully taken for the purpose of quelling a riot or insurrection.*

Article 2(1)

8.4 The first sentence of article 2(1) places a positive obligation on those who make law to ensure that they protect the right to life.[2]

---

1 For a more detailed examination see K Starmer, *European Human Rights Law* (1999, Legal Action Group). New edition forthcoming 2008.
2 Positive obligations are examined in detail at paras 9.19 – 9.29.

8.5   The second sentence of article 2(1) places a negative duty on public authorities to refrain from intentionally or unlawfully interfering with a person's right to life. The exception concerning the use of the death penalty has been superseded following the signing of Optional Protocol 6 by the UK.[3]

8.6   The positive obligation on public authorities in the second sentence of article 2(1) goes further than the duty to put effective criminal law provisions in place to protect life. It extends the duty to protect witnesses and informants and to places a duty on those who run, for example, care homes, hospitals, prisons or detention centres to take appropriate steps to protect and safeguard the life of a person. Where a person dies, there is a duty on those who knew or ought to have known at the time of the existence of a real and immediate risk to that person to take measures within the scope of their powers which, judged reasonably, might have been expected to avoid that risk.[4]

Case illustration

D was arrested for armed robbery. He gave statements and evidence against the other parties involved. Police intelligence identified that D's life was in danger and he was placed in the prison's protected witness unit. D was attacked twice following his release from prison and also went on to commit further serious offences for which he was imprisoned. On his return to prison he was refused entry into the protected witness unit because it was felt that there was no evidence or intelligence to suggest that his life was still under threat. The prison service was found to be at fault because it did not assess whether there was a real risk to the life of the prisoner if he was not admitted into a protected witness unit and to determine whether this was a present and continuing risk.[5]

8.7   If a person, while in an institution, such as a prison, mental health hospital or residential care home, dies unexpectedly, by suicide or at the hands of another individual, public authorities are under a

---

3 See below at para 8.145.
4 *Osman v UK* (1999) 29 EHRR 245.
5 *R v Chief Constable of Norfolk Police and others ex p DF* [2002] EWHC 1738.

positive obligation to ensure that an effective, thorough and impartial investigation is conducted into the death.

Case illustration

The family of a prisoner who died following a severe asthma attack complained about the lack of a thorough, independent and public investigation and the failure by the authorities to provide them with proper information as to the reasons for the death. The court held that there was a duty to carry out an effective investigation which included the calling of witness and independent expert evidence.[6]

Article 2(2)

8.8 Article 2(2)(a)–(c) sets out the limited situations in which the use of force resulting in death will not contravene the right to life. A high test is required to justify such lethal force. The authorities do not simply have to balance the individual right with the public interest. They must establish that the action was absolutely necessary in the circumstances.

Case illustration

In an operation that resulted in the killing of three IRA suspects by the SAS, the European Court considered whether the operation was planned and controlled by the authorities in a way that minimised, to the greatest extent possible, recourse to legal force.[7]

8.9 Where lethal force is used by the authorities, a thorough, effective and impartial investigation must follow into the use of force. This may not only concern the actions of those directly responsible for death but, where relevant, the training, planning and organisation that those carrying out the act are given.

---

6 *R on the application of Margaret Wright v Secretary of State for the Home Department* [2002] HRLR 1.

7 *McCann v UK* (1995) 21 EHRR 97.

Case illustration

The investigation into the shooting of the IRA suspects by the SAS was not to be limited to the actions of those agents who carried out the killing, but also had to consider the planning of the operation by those in command to ensure that no more force was used than was absolutely necessary.[8]

Areas of interest under Article 2

Abortion

8.10   The right to life does not require a country to prohibit abortion. Although it is accepted that the unborn foetus may have certain limited rights, it does not have an absolute right to life, as it cannot be regarded in isolation from the pregnant woman. The European Court recognised that it is possible to allow a mother to terminate pregnancy where physical well-being, mental health or even social reasons exist.[9]

8.11   The rights of the unborn foetus are also closely linked to the article 8 right to respect for the private life of the mother and, to a lesser extent, the father. Whenever a woman is pregnant her private life will become closely connected with the developing foetus. However, the termination of a pregnancy is not solely a matter of private life for the mother. All reasonable legal rules restricting abortion will not be regarded as violating the mother's right to termination.[10]

8.12   The father of an unborn child has the right to raise issues on his or the unborn child's behalf, but does not have a right to insist that the child be born against the wishes of the mother.[11]

Euthanasia

8.13   There are two types of euthanasia recognised in law, active and passive euthanasia.

---

8   Ibid.

9   *See H v Norway* (1992) App No 17004/90 (unreported). This case can be found on the Council of Europe website.

10   *Bruggemann & Sheuten v Germany* (1976) 5 DR 103.

11   *Paton v UK* (1980) 19 DR 244.

8.14   Active euthanasia is sometimes referred to as assisted suicide. It concerns a situation where a person who does not rely on life-saving equipment for their continued existence requests that the authorities take active steps or allow someone else to actively take steps to kill them as they are incapable of carrying out the act by themselves. Public authorities do not contravene their responsibilities under the right to life by refusing to assist that person or allow another to assist with their death.

Case illustration

A person suffering from an incurable degenerative disease faced an undignified death through respiratory failure. There is no law in the UK against suicide; however, the person was unable to die without assistance from another. She sought a declaration from the court that her husband, who she wanted to assist her, would not be prosecuted for his involvement in her death. The European Court found that, in situations where a country does not permit assisted suicides, the Court is not concerned with a person's quality of life. Nor could it create an entitlement to choose death rather than life. Accordingly, this meant that there is no right to die at the hands of a third person or with the assistance of a public authority.[12]

8.15   However, the situation with respect to passive euthanasia is different. The issue may be raised where a person is only kept alive by a machine and will die if that medical intervention is stopped. If in these narrow circumstances, the patient, being of sound mind (or those who may lawfully take the decision on their behalf) decides that they wish to withdraw their consent to the life-continuing treatment, the authorities are not under a duty to prolong life where it is not in the interests of that patient.

---

12 *See Pretty v UK* (2002) 35 EHRR 1.

Case illustration

A seriously disabled patient with mental capacity who was kept alive by a ventilator was entitled to request that it be turned off.[13] The hospital had no power to refuse her request.

The treatment of the terminally ill

8.16   It has been decided that where responsible medical officers take the view that treatment is no longer in the interests of the patient it does not have a duty to prolong life and can, therefore, withdraw artificial nutrition and hydration that will bring about the person's death. In these circumstances, such a decision is not regarded as violating the right to life because it is based on decision not to do something rather than a decision to carry out a deliberate action.

Case illustrations

The withdrawal of food for a patient in a persistent vegetative state was not regarded as a breach of Article 2.[14]

B suffered from a degenerative condition that would eventually result in the need for artificial nutrition and hydration. He wished to continue receiving artificial nutrition and hydration and wanted to be assured that doctors would not withdraw this artificial hydration and nutrition as he did not want to die of hunger and thirst. The evidence showed that B should remain able to make rational decisions about himself and his treatment until a period very shortly before his death. The Court confirmed that where a competent patient indicated his or her wish to be kept alive in such a way, any doctor who deliberately brought the patient's life to an end by discontinuing this supply would not only be in breach of duty but guilty of murder. The Court also confirmed that where a dying patient is incompetent, a doctor was not under a duty to continue artificial nutrition and hydration where it was not considered in the incompetent patient's best interests to be

---

13   *B v An NHS Hospital Trust* (2002) 65 BMLR 149.
14   *NHS Trust A v M* [2001] 2 WLR 942.

kept alive. The Court found that the General Medical Council (GMC) guidelines were able to protect B's rights in his situation and concluded by highlighting the responsibility of the GMC to ensure that this guidance was understood and implemented at every level of the NHS. It emphasised that patients and, in particular, those who suffer from a disability are entitled to have confidence that they will be treated properly and in accordance with good practice, and that they will not be ignored or patronised because of their disability.[15]

Article 3 – prohibition of torture

No one shall be subjected to torture or to inhuman or degrading treatment or punishment.

8.17 Article 3 places a negative duty on states not to subject individuals to any of the following three separate categories of ill treatment:

- Degrading treatment or punishment will occur where a person deliberately or unintentionally feels fear, anguish and inferiority that is humiliating and debasing.
- Inhuman treatment or punishment will occur when intense physical and mental suffering are caused whether deliberately or unintentionally.
- Torture occurs when there is deliberate inhuman treatment causing very serious and cruel suffering.

8.18 A wide range of circumstances must be considered before it is determined whether this right has been violated. These include the age, sex and state of health of the victim, the duration of the treatment and its physical and mental effects. A further factor to be considered will be the circumstances in which the treatment is carried out. For instance, a person convicted of a crime may feel degraded by their imprisonment or community service sentence, but this will not make it contrary to article 3. In contrast, the non-availability of state support for asylum seekers as soon as it was

15 *R on the application of Burke v General Medical Council and others* [2005] 3 WLR 1132.

made clear that there was an immediate prospect of a breach of article 3 placed the state under a duty to avoid it.[16]

8.19   The obligation not to interfere with the article 3 right may need to be put in context with the obligation on states to protect the right to life under article 2. This may be relevant for the health care of a patient.

Case illustration

The decision by prison authorities to force feed a prisoner who was on hunger strike did not amount to inhuman or degrading treatment since it was carried out in accordance with the positive obligation on the state to protect life.[17] However, if the treatment is for a medical necessity, the authorities must show that the medical necessity exists.[18]

8.20   It is up to the person claiming a violation with respect to article 3 to prove beyond any reasonable doubt that the public sector organisations, or those charities or private bodies carrying out public functions were responsible for their ill treatment. However, if a person leaves, for example, a police station, hospital or care home with certain unexplained injuries, the onus will be on the authorities to explain why they are not responsible.

Case illustration

Where a person entered into police custody in good health, but was found to be injured at the time of release, the detaining body was under a duty to provide a plausible explanation as to the cause of the injury.[19]

8.21   Those who have responsibility for the running of institutions may be responsible for unauthorised acts by members of staff, even where

---

16   R on the application of Limbuela and others v Secretary of State for the Home Department [2005] 3 WLR 1014.

17   X v FRG (1985) 7 EHRR 152.

18   R on the application of Wilkinson v RMO Broadmoor [2002] 1 WLR 419.

19   Selmouni v France (1999) 29 EHRR 403.

the acts are performed without express authorisation, and even outside or against instructions.

Case illustration

In a case where interrogation techniques were used to force confessions, the European Court found that it was inconceivable that the higher authorities were unaware or, at least entitled to be unaware of the existence of such practice. Those authorities are strictly liable for the conduct of their subordinates and are under a duty to ensure that they impose standards upon them. They cannot shelter behind their inability to ensure that their will is respected.[20]

8.22 In addition to their duty not to act in a way that violates the article 3 rights of another person, public sector organisations as well as charities or public bodies which carry out public functions in the running of, for example, residential, security or healthcare centres, have certain positive obligations under article 3.

8.23 These positive obligations include:

- A duty to prevent breaches of article 3.

Case illustration

The failure of a local authority to separate four children from their mother even though it was clear that the children were being subjected to a quite unacceptable level of abuse and neglect placed it in violation of its duty to prevent such breaches.[21]

---

20 *Ireland v UK* (1980) 2 EHRR 25.
21 *Z v UK* (2002) 34 EHRR 97.

- A duty to investigate a violation of article 3.

> **Case illustration**
>
> The European Court found that there was a need for an effective official investigation into allegations of police ill treatment.[22]

8.24   There is a duty on any public sector organisation, as well as charities or private bodies which carry out public functions in the running of, for example, residential, security or healthcare centres, to provide services or resources that will be sufficient to prevent a person from being treated in a manner that amounts to inhuman or degrading treatment.

> **Case illustration**
>
> The sending to prison of a quadriplegic woman for refusing to pay a debt was not, of itself in contravention of article 3. However, the fact that the authorities detained her when they did not have the appropriate facilities for a person with her disability did amount to degrading treatment in violation of the Convention.[23]

8.25   There is a duty to provide effective criminal laws to prohibit acts by individuals which amount to a violation of article 3.

> **Case illustration**
>
> The European Court found that the failure of the law to adequately protect a child from being beaten by his stepfather with a garden rake contravened article 3.[24]

---

22   *Assenov v Bulgaria* (1998) 28 EHRR 652.
23   *Price v UK* (2001) 11 BHRC 401; (2002) 5 CCLR 306.
24   *A v UK* (1998) 27 EHRR 611.

Article 4 – prohibition of slavery and forced labour

(1) No one shall be held in slavery or servitude.

(2) No one shall be required to perform forced or compulsory labour.

(3) For the purpose of this article the term 'forced or compulsory labour' shall not include:

> *(a) any work required to be done in the ordinary course of detention imposed according to the provisions of article 5 of this Convention or during conditional release from such detention;*

> *(b) any service of a military character or, in case of conscientious objectors in countries where they are recognised, service exacted instead of compulsory military service;*

> *(c) any service exacted in case of an emergency or calamity threatening the life or well-being of the community;*

> *(d) any work or service which forms part of normal civic obligations.*

Article 4(1)

8.26 Slavery means the status or condition of a person over whom any or all of the powers attaching to the rights of ownership are exercised.

8.27 Servitude is a particularly serious form of denial of freedom where the person is obliged to live on another's property and it is impossible to change this condition.[25]

Case illustration

A girl, S, was brought into a country on the understanding that her immigration status would be regularised and that she would receive education. S was subsequently 'lent' to another family where she was used as an unpaid servant against her will. Despite the family's promises, S was not sent to school and could not leave the family for fear of arrest because her papers had been confiscated. The Court held that this treatment amounted to servitude. It did not consider the treatment to be slavery as the family did not exercise a real right of ownership over S.

---

25 The distinction between 'slavery' and 'servitude' was considered in the case of *Siliadin v France* App no 73316/01 (see case illustration below).

Article 4(2)

8.28   Forced labour is work carried out under physical or mental constraint, while compulsory labour is effectively work performed under the menace of a penalty and against the will of a person concerned. Forced or compulsory labour is a much broader concept concerned with work exacted under threat of a penalty.

Article 4(3)

8.29   This defines the scope of article 4(2). It establishes exceptions to forced or compulsory labour. For instance, work aimed at the rehabilitation of prisoners or their reintegration into society will not contravene article 4. Nor will compulsory national service, so long as those who object to military service are given the opportunity to carry out some substitute type of service.

Article 5 – right to liberty and security

(1) *Everyone has the right to liberty and security of person. No one shall be deprived of his liberty save in the following cases and in accordance with a procedure prescribed by law:*

(a) *the lawful detention of a person after conviction by a competent court;*

(b) *the lawful arrest or detention of a person for non-compliance with the lawful order of a court or in order to secure the fulfilment of any obligation prescribed by law;*

(c) *the lawful arrest or detention of a person effected for the purpose of bringing him before the competent legal authority on reasonable suspicion of having committed an offence or when it is reasonably considered necessary to prevent his committing an offence or fleeing after having done so;*

(d) *the detention of a minor by lawful order for the purpose of educational supervision or his lawful detention for the purpose of bringing him before the competent legal authority;*

(e) *the lawful detention of persons for the prevention of the spreading of infectious diseases, of persons of unsound mind, alcoholics or drug addicts or vagrants;*

(f) *the lawful arrest or detention of a person to prevent his effecting an unauthorised entry into the country or of a person against whom action is being taken with a view to deportation or extradition.*

(2) *Everyone who is arrested shall be informed promptly, in a language which he understands, of the reasons for his arrest and of any charge against him.*

(3) *Everyone arrested or detained in accordance with the provisions of paragraph (1)(c) of this article shall be brought promptly before a judge or other officer authorised by law to exercise judicial power and shall be entitled to trial within a reasonable time or to release pending trial. Release may be conditioned by guarantees to appear for trial.*

(4) *Everyone who is deprived of his liberty by arrest or detention shall be entitled to take proceedings by which the lawfulness of his detention shall be decided speedily by a court and his release ordered if the detention is not lawful.*

(5) *Everyone who has been the victim of arrest or detention in contravention of the provisions of this article shall have an enforceable right to compensation.*

8.30   This article is concerned with the circumstances in which a person may be detained by public authorities. Whether restrictions placed on a person's right to move about freely amount to a deprivation will be based on the degree of the restriction and the reason why it is being imposed.[26]

Article 5(1)(a) – (f)

8.31   Everyone has a right not to be detained against their will. However, it is accepted that deprivation of liberty amounts to a legitimate form of social control over persons within the jurisdiction. A deprivation of liberty is permitted for one of a limited number of reasons set out in article 5(1)(a) – (f). In order to be legitimate, article 5(1) states that a deprivation of liberty must be in accordance with a procedure carried out by law.[27] The European Court has made clear that the notion of lawfulness implies more than just compliance with domestic law; it also prohibits detention if it is arbitrary. Therefore, just because a deprivation of liberty can be carried out in accordance with domestic law does not necessarily mean that it will not be arbitrary. Arbitrariness is interpreted to include elements of inappropriateness, bad faith or injustice.[28]

26 *Guzzardi v Italy* (1981) 3 EHRR 333.
27 See paras 10.13 – 10.18 for a more detailed consideration of the meaning of 'a procedure carried out by law'.
28 As well as the case illustrations, below see the case of *Bozano v France* below at note 41.

Case illustrations

A person (HL) was admitted to a psychiatric hospital under the common law doctrine of necessity by two doctors who believed that this was in his 'best interests'. HL was severely disabled and lacked capacity. He was not capable of requesting that he be released from the hospital. The UK courts decided that HL was not being formally detained under the Mental Health Act 1983 and so he was not able to rely on the legal safeguards that automatically apply to people detained under the Act in order to ensure that detention is appropriate, The European Court found that HL had been deprived of his liberty and that his detention was unlawful because the common law of doctrine of necessity contained insufficient safeguards to protect him from arbitrary or mistaken detention. It was, therefore, found to be a violation of Article 5(1).[29]

The indefinite detention of non-British nationals without charge under Part 4 of the Anti-Terrorism Crime and Security Act 2001 was found to be arbitrary in a case decided in the House of Lords. These non-British nationals could not be removed to another country because of the risk of being subjected to torture in violation of Article 3 of the European Convention. The Court recognised that, as well as the foreign nationals, there are a number of UK nationals who also presented a risk to national security. However, they were not detained because the authorities believed that their activities could be adequately monitored without the need to detain them. There was no justification for this differential treatment. Therefore, the House of Lords concluded that the detention of the non-British nationals was arbitrary and in violation of Article 5 (and 14).[30]

8.32   The limitations in article 5(1) refer to the following situations:
(a)   A person can be detained following a conviction by a court or tribunal that has the authority to hear the case.

---

29   *HL v UK* (2004) 40 EHRR 761.
30   *A v Secretary of State for the Home Department* [2005] 2 WLR 87.

(b) A person can be detained if they do not comply with a specific obligation from a previous court order. It has been accepted that in narrow circumstances, so far confined to anti-terrorist legislation, a person may be detained at a port or airport to answer questions even though they have not been given the opportunity to comply with a specific obligation.[31]

(c) A person can be detained in order to be brought before a court on reasonable suspicion of having committed a criminal offence. It authorises the detention of a person from committing a specific offence (this means that there can be no general policy of preventative detention) or fleeing after having committed one.

(d) This has two elements. The first entitles a child to be detained in accordance with a court order that aims to secure their attendance at an educational establishment. The second provides for a child to be detained in order to remove them from harmful surroundings, for example, detention pending a court order placing a child in care. This does not cover the child who is detained for a criminal offence (which is covered under article 5(1)(c)).

(e) This is designed for the individual's own protection and for the protection of the public.

The meaning of 'unsound mind'

8.33 The term 'unsound mind' has not been given a definitive meaning because it is sensitive to evolving medical and psychiatric understanding. In order to justify a detention, there will need to be reliable evidence from an objective medical expert and the disorder must be of a kind or degree that warrants detention.[32]

8.34 Detention in an institution may be lawful even if the patient could live in the community if properly supported, so long as the patient comes within the 'unsound mind' definition.[33]

8.35 The continued detention of a person who is no longer of unsound mind is unlawful. However, where a person who was initially deprived of their liberty due to mental illness, is subsequently detained to protect the public from serious harm, the detention will

---

31 *McVeigh, O'Neill & Evans v UK* (1983) 5 EHRR 71.

32 *Winterwerp v Netherlands* (1980) 2 EHRR 387.

33 See *R on the application of K v Camden and Islington Health Authority* [2001] 3 WLR 553.

be lawful so long as the underlying mental illness subsists, even if it is no longer treatable.[34]

8.36   It is contrary to article 5, to place the burden of proof on a detained person to prove they no longer suffer from a mental disorder which justifies their detention.[35]

The meaning of 'alcoholic'

8.37   The term 'alcoholic' has been extended by the court to include those who are moderately intoxicated. However, in all cases the person must pose a threat to themselves or the public.[36]

The meaning of 'vagrant'

8.38   The term 'vagrant' has been defined by the European Court as a person of no fixed abode, no means of subsistence and no trade or profession.[37]

(f) Detention in determining a person's asylum claim or their deportation will only be justified for as long as asylum or deportation proceedings are in progress.

Case illustration

The decision to detain a person in a 'reception centre' is lawful even if there is no risk of the person absconding, where it is designed to facilitate a speedy determination of asylum cases. It ensures that asylum-seekers are available for interview at all times.[38]

8.39   However, excessive delay or the failure to deal with asylum or deportation proceedings diligently may render the detention unlawful.[39] Furthermore, detention will only be justified so long as

---

34   *Anderson v Scottish Ministers* 8 BHRC 589.
35   *R on the application of H v Mental Health Review Tribunal, North and East London Region* [2001] 3 WLR 512.
36   *Witold Litwa v Poland* (2000) 33 EHRR 1267.
37   *De Wilde, Ooms & Versyp v Belgium* (1979) 1 EHRR 373.
38   See *R v Secretary of State for the Home Department ex p Shayan Baram Saadi and others* [2002] 1 WLR 3131.
39   See *Chahal v UK* (1997) 23 EHRR 413.

deportation or extradition proceedings are in progress. Where the deportation or extradition is not possible, a person cannot be detained under article 5(1)(f).[40]

8.40   The fact that proceedings are subsequently found to be unlawful does not affect the legality of the detention while it occurred. However, the need to act in accordance with the law means that deportation or extradition cannot be carried out in an arbitrary manner.

Case illustration

A person had been tried and convicted by the Italian courts in his absence and sentenced to life imprisonment for murder. The person was subsequently arrested in France. He could not be extradited back to Italy because French extradition laws did not recognise convictions where a person was tried in their absence. Therefore, the French authorities arrested the individual and drove him to the French/Swiss border where he was handed over to the Swiss authorities. Since the Swiss extradition laws recognised a conviction where a person is tried in their absence, the individual could be extradited to Italy. However, the arrest by the French authorities was found to be arbitrary as it was used to overcome the inability of the French authorities to extradite the individual from France.[41]

Article 5(2)

8.41   This concerns the right of a person to be informed of the reason for their detention. It states that any person who is arrested or detained must be told in simple, clear, non-technical language essentially why they are being lawfully deprived of their liberty. The purpose of this is to allow a person to apply to a court to challenge the lawfulness of their detention.

8.42   If this cannot be given at the moment when the person is being detained it should be given within a sufficient period following arrest.

---

40 However, see derogation case illustration at para 9.33.
41 *Bozano v France* (1986) 9 EHRR 297.

Article 5(3)

8.43   This provision relates solely to article 5(1)(c) and, therefore, only applies to criminal offences. It guarantees the right of a person to be brought promptly before a judge or other person who is authorised to exercise judicial power, invariably a magistrates' court. It also entitles the person to be released on bail unless there are factual reasons why their detention should continue. Where a person has been refused bail, their case should be given priority by the prosecution and the court.

Article 5(4)

8.44   Every person deprived of their liberty can take proceedings in order to have the lawfulness of their detention decided speedily by the court. The person's release will be ordered if the detention is not lawful. This is sometimes referred to as the right to habeas corpus. A person must have speedy access to a review about the necessity of their detention, and any remedy must be implemented quickly.

8.45   A review by a court or tribunal under article 5(4) applies where the initial decision to detain a person was not made by a court or a tribunal. For instance, a person who is remanded in custody for a criminal offence will require short intervals between reviews. This provision also applies where the reasons for detaining a person may change over time, such as in circumstances where a person is detained on mental health grounds that may change.

Article 5(5)

8.46   This specifically provides for a right to compensation where article 5 has been breached.

Article 6 – right to a fair trial

(1) In the determination of his civil rights and obligations or of any criminal charge against him, everyone is entitled to a fair and public hearing within a reasonable time by an independent and impartial tribunal established by law. Judgment shall be pronounced publicly but the press and public may be excluded from all or part of the trial in the interests of morals, public order or national security in a

democratic society, where the interests of juveniles or the protection of the private life of the parties so require, or to the extent strictly necessary in the opinion of the court in special circumstances where publicity would prejudice the interests of justice.

(2) Everyone charged with a criminal offence shall be presumed innocent until proved guilty according to law.

(3) Everyone charged with a criminal offence has the following minimum rights:

(a) to be informed promptly, in a language which he understands and in detail, of the nature and cause of the accusation against him;

(b) to have adequate time and facilities for the preparation of his defence;

(c) to defend himself in person or through legal assistance of his own choosing or, if he has not sufficient means to pay for legal assistance, to be given it free when the interests of justice so require;

(d) to examine or have examined witnesses against him and to obtain the attendance and examination of witnesses on his behalf under the same conditions as witnesses against him;

(e) to have the free assistance of an interpreter if he cannot understand or speak the language used in court.

8.47 A person is entitled to rely on fair trial provisions in relation to criminal and civil proceedings. Criminal fair trial rights are more extensive than civil fair trial rights. While the provisions contained in article 6(1) relate to both, article 6(2) and (3) apply only to criminal proceedings. However, some of the rights which are included in the criminal fair trial provisions have been implied into civil fair trial provisions.

8.48 The analysis of article 6 will concentrate on civil fair trial rights since they are of greater relevance to this book.

The right to a fair trial in civil proceedings

8.49 The right to a fair trial in civil proceedings must be considered in two stages. Before considering the content of the fair trial rights, it is necessary to establish whether the right to a fair trial exists for the situation in question. In order for a civil fair trial right to apply three pre-conditions must be met. The first is that the right or obligation in question must be 'civil' in nature. The second is that the right must have a basis in UK law. Finally, there must be a need for a 'determination' of the right or obligation in question. These three factors will be defined below.

The meaning of 'civil rights and obligations'

8.50 It is for the courts to determine whether a case concerns the determination of a civil right or obligation. In doing so, it will look at the character of the right in question rather than accepting its classification under domestic law.[42] The approach of the European Court has been to look at each case on its facts. The term 'civil rights and obligation' has proved difficult to define, not least because its meaning has developed through case law of the European Court which has not always been clear or seemingly consistent.

8.51 'Civil rights and obligations' include all types of ordinary civil litigation between private individuals, such as contract law, tort law, property law, family law, employment law. Therefore, the UK courts must ensure that the fair trial measures in article 6(1) are applied to any dispute between individuals and/or private bodies.

8.52 The complications occur in situations which involve the relationship between an individual or private body and a public authority, since the right to a fair trial applies to some but not all disputes between these parties. In determining where the divide lies, the crucial factor has been a consideration of the personal, economic or individual characteristics of such a dispute. Where such characteristics predominate, the proceedings are likely to be covered by article 6(1), irrespective of whether they are regarded as private or public law proceedings under UK law.

8.53 It is not possible to set out a definitive framework that the European Court applies in order to establish whether the personal, economic or individual characteristics of a particular dispute have predominated. Therefore, this section will look at situations where the European Court has decided that article 6(1) should apply and those where it has decided they should not.

It has been established that article 6(1) rights apply to the following disputes between individuals and private bodies and public authorities:

Property disputes

8.54 Most proceedings which have a bearing on property rights are considered to be 'civil rights and obligations' if they have a direct

42 See para 10.7.

impact on the owner of the property. This includes planning procedures, such as those concerning building permits,[43] and confiscation of property.[44] It also includes proceedings where the outcome impacts on the use or enjoyment of the property.[45] Intellectual property rights are also regarded as 'civil rights' as is the entitlement to compensation for breaches of property rights, but not before a patent has been registered.

Licensing decisions which affect a profession or the right to engage in commercial activity

8.55 These include the right to practice a profession,[46] withdrawal of an alcohol licence from a restaurant,[47] and permission to run a school.[48]

Family proceedings

8.56 These include decisions to place a child in care,[49] parental access to a child in care,[50] adoption and fostering.[51]

Compensation from public authorities

8.57 These include damages against public authorities which are based in contract,[52] damages caused by medical negligence in a hospital,[53] and unlawful detention following the wrongful issue of an arrest warrant.[54] Article 6(1) rights were also engaged following an unlawful refusal to grant a manufacturing licence.[55]

Claims for welfare benefits

8.58 The general rule is that article 6(1) rights are engaged for a person who is entitled to a benefit, such as welfare allowances, for example,

---

43 *Sporrong & Lonroth v Sweden* (1984) 7 EHRR 256.
44 *Raimondo v Italy* (1994) 18 EHRR 237.
45 *Zander v Sweden* (1994) 18 EHRR 175.
46 *Konig v Germany* (1978) 2 EHRR 170.
47 *Tre Traktorer v Sweden* (1991) 13 EHRR 309.
48 *Jordebro Foundation of Christian Schools v Sweden* (1987) 61 DR 92.
49 *Olsson v Sweden* (No 1) (1988) 11 EHRR 259.
50 *W v UK* (1987) 10 EHRR 29.
51 *Keegan v Ireland* (1994) 18 EHRR 342; *Eriksson v Sweden* (1989) 12 EHRR 183.
52 *Stran Greek Refineries and Stratis Andreadis v Greece* (1994) 19 EHRR 293.
53 *H v France* (1990) 12 EHRR 74.
54 *Baraona v Portugal* (1991) 13 EHRR 329.
55 *Neves e Silva v Portugal* (1991) 13 EHRR 535.

disability benefits, health insurance benefits and state pensions.[56] However, where the payment of benefits that the person is claiming is discretionary, the general understanding is that fair trial rights do not apply.[57]

Alternatively, it has been established that article 6(1) fair trial rights do not apply to the following disputes between individuals or private bodies and public authorities:[58]

Taxation issues

8.59   Strasbourg has consistently held that article 6(1) does not apply to tax proceedings, such as claims for the right to tax reimbursements.[59] However, this does not include the right to recover monies paid in tax, where the regulations under which the tax was paid are later declared invalid.[60]

Discretionary or ex gratia payments

8.60   Article 6(1) does not apply to these payments because the individual or private body has no 'right' to such a payment.

Immigration and nationality issues

8.61   Even though there are cases where decisions on these issues will clearly affect a person's civil rights, no 'right' appears to exist for those without citizenship status in a country.

Employment disputes between public servants and their employers

8.62   Article 6(1) rights do not apply to disputes relating to the recruitment, employment and retirement of public servants, such as the police or armed forces.[61]

State education

8.63   The right to state education is regarded as a 'public law' rather than a 'private' right. Accordingly, article 6(1) does not apply to procedures

---

56 *Schuler-Zgraggen v Switzerland* (1993) 16 EHRR 405.
57 *Machatova v Slovak Republic* (1997) 24 EHRR CD 44.
58 Challenges may still be brought for violations of other Convention rights.
59 *X v Austria* (1980) 21 DR 246.
60 *National & Provincial Building Society and others v UK* (1998) 25 EHRR 127 – this would come under compensation from public authorities (above).
61 *Pellegrin v France* (2001) 31 EHRR 26.

concerning the schooling of children with special educational needs.[62]

Election rights

8.64 The right to stand for election is regarded as a political rather than a civil right.[63] As a result article 6(1) does not apply.

The right must have a basis in domestic law

8.65 Article 6(1) regulates the manner in which those civil rights and obligations recognised in domestic law are to be applied. The European Court will only apply fair trial rights where an individual or private body has, at least, an arguable claim to a civil right or obligation under domestic law.

8.66 One area that has proved problematic is whether to recognise immunities from legal action which would otherwise be accepted as a civil right.[64]

The need for a determination of the right or obligation

8.67 In order for there to be a need for a 'determination' of a civil right or obligation, the dispute must be one that is genuine and of a serious nature.[65] This means that the dispute must be based on actual facts and not hypothetical ones. In addition, article 6(1) will not be applied when there is only a remote or tenuous link between the proceedings and the effect it may have on a civil right or obligation.[66]

The content of article 6(1)

8.68 Article 6(1) is not only concerned with express rights contained in the text of the Convention. The European Court has also found it necessary to read in particular rights in order to ensure that the effectiveness of the provisions.[67]

---

62 *Simpson v UK* (1989) 64 DR 188.
63 *Pierre-Bloch v France* (1998) 26 EHRR 202.
64 See para 10.44.
65 *Van Marle v Netherlands* (1986) 8 EHRR 483.
66 *Pudas v Hungary* (1988) 10 EHRR 380.
67 See para 9.15.

Rights expressly set out in article 6(1)

A public hearing

8.69   Civil proceedings should take place in public. However, article 6(1) expressly sets out a list of exceptions which help to define the scope of the general rule. The press or public may be excluded from some or all of a trial:

(a)   in the interests of morals;

(b)   public order;

(c)   national security;

(d)   where the interests of juveniles or the protection of the private life of the parties so require;

(e)   to the extent strictly necessary in the opinion of the court in special circumstances where publicity would prejudice the interests of justice.

8.70   These reasons are to be strictly applied, and it must be ensured that they are proportionate to the objective they are trying to achieve.[68]

8.71   The need for a private hearing has been justified in cases concerning sexual offences against children, divorce proceedings, medical disciplinary proceedings to protect a patient's privacy and prison disciplinary hearings where they affect public order and security.

An independent and impartial tribunal established by law

8.72   A tribunal must be independent of the government and the parties to the action. In determining whether the requirement is met, relevant factors include:

(a)   the manner of appointment;

(b)   safeguards against outside pressure;

(c)   an appearance of independence. This not only means that there must be no bias but a lack of the appearance of bias.

8.73   The reference to a 'tribunal established by law' means that the tribunal will need to have judicial functions, fair procedures and be capable of making a binding determination. The power to simply make recommendations is not enough.

Trial within a reasonable period

8.74   This is designed to protect all parties to court proceedings against excessive procedural delay. Time usually starts to run from the

68   See paras 10.19 – 10.26.

initiation of legal proceedings; this is usually through a claim form filed at the court. There is no fixed period of time which is regarded as reasonable. Relevant factors include, the complexity of the case, what is at stake, the conduct of the parties and the conduct of the court.

Publicly pronounced judgment

8.75   This does not mean that the judgment needs to be read out in open court. The judgment will be regarded as accessible so long as written notification is provided to the parties.

Rights that have been read into article 6(1)

8.76   Three rights have been implied into the Convention. The right to participate effectively in proceedings and to legal representation have a particularly close link.

The right of access to a court

8.77   This has been read into the Convention, since the right to a fair trial would be meaningless if an individual does not have access to a court.

8.78   However, as with other implied rights, it is subject to restrictions because there is a duty on the government to regulate access to court so that there is a fair balance between the individual right and a consideration of the interests of the community, including resource implications. Access to court may be restricted for vexatious litigants, children, bankrupts and those suffering mental illness among others. However, any restriction must have a legitimate aim and be proportionate since access to court cannot be denied if it impairs the essence of the right.[69]

8.79   Access to court may be waived by agreeing to arbitration. However, all parties must freely and voluntarily enter into the arbitration process. A public authority may also be able to rely on immunity from legal action.[70]

Right to legal representation

8.80   Unlike criminal proceedings (see article 6(3)(c)) there is no express right to legal aid in civil cases. The European Court has implied the right into article 6(1). However, legal aid will not automatically be

69   See para 10.26.
70   See para 10.44.

provided where a person cannot afford legal representation. The implied right is limited to cases where the courts consider legal assistance to be necessary given such factors as, the complexity of the law and the capacity of the individual to represent themselves. They will also consider whether there is any prospect of success.

Right to participate effectively in proceedings

8.81   The courts will need to determine whether the proceedings, when considered as a whole, are fair and that the rights of the parties are adequately respected. Effective participation is guaranteed by the following cluster of implied rights:

(a)   The right to equality of arms. This means that every party to an action should be provided with a reasonable opportunity to present their case under conditions that do not place them at a substantial disadvantage to their opponent.

(b)   The right to an adversarial hearing. This refers to the right to call and challenge evidence and to address

(c)   Disclosure. All relevant documents to the civil proceedings should be disclosed by the parties prior to a trial.

(d)   Evidence. Parties must have a proper opportunity to call and examine witnesses. This may include the right to call expert witnesses as well as witnesses who will testify on the facts of the case.

Fair trial guarantees in criminal proceedings

8.82   When determining whether an offence is a criminal or a civil one, the European Court has set out three criteria. Firstly, it will see how the proceedings are classified in the domestic law. Secondly, it will look at the nature of the offence and the conduct in question. Finally, it will look at the severity of any possible penalty.

8.83   Article 6(1) requires that there be a public (with certain exceptions) hearing by an independent and impartial tribunal. The trial should take place within a reasonable time and culminate in a public judgment giving a reasoned decision. The right of access to court and to participate effectively into proceedings have also been implied into the right.

8.84   Article 6(2) highlights the importance of the presumption that a person is innocent of a crime until proven guilty.

8.85   Article 6(3) expressly states that a person accused of a crime is told why they are being charged. They must also be given adequate time and facilities to prepare a defence and legally aided representation should they need it. At trial the defendant has the right to call and cross-examine witnesses (although the court has implied certain restrictions into this right) and to an interpreter at court should one be needed. The Court has also implied that a defendant should have the right to silence during questioning and at trial. This is often referred to as 'freedom from self-incrimination', although inferences can be drawn from this silence.

Article 7 – no punishment without law

(1) No one shall be held guilty of any criminal offence on account of any act or omission which did not constitute a criminal offence under national or international law at the time when it was committed. Nor shall a heavier penalty be imposed than the one that was applicable at the time the criminal offence was committed.

(2) This article shall not prejudice the trial and punishment of any person for any act or omission which, at the time when it was committed, was criminal according to the general principles of law recognised by civilised nations.

Article 7(1)

8.86   This section applies to criminal offences only. It states that criminal law should not be applied retrospectively. The law must be sufficiently accessible and foreseeable in order to apply to a defendant.[71] In addition, no heavier penalty can be imposed following conviction than was allowed at the time when the act was committed.

Article 7(2)

8.87   A person may be tried retrospectively for an offence if it is one that would be regarded as criminal under the general principles of international law.

---

71 See paras 10.17 – 10.18.

> **Case illustration**
>
> The War Crimes Act 1991 is an example of retrospective legislation passed in order to bring to trial any persons living in the UK who had been involved with crimes against humanity on German or German-occupied territories during the Second World War.

Article 8 – right to respect for private and family life

(1) *Everyone has the right to respect for his private and family life, his home and his correspondence.*

(2) *There shall be no interference by a public authority with the exercise of this right except such as is in accordance with the law and is necessary in a democratic society in the interests of national security, public safety or the economic well-being of the country, for the prevention of disorder or crime, for the protection of health or morals, or for the protection of the rights and freedoms of others.*

Article 8(1)

8.88   The right to respect for privacy relates to a person's:

- private life;
- family life;
- home; and
- correspondence.

Private life

8.89   The notion of private life is broad and the European Court has emphasised that it is not susceptible to exhaustive definition. It has long been recognised that the right to private life is concerned with an 'inner circle' within which individuals should be able to live their own personal life as they choose and exclude the outside world not encompassed within that circle. However, the right to private life is also recognised as extending beyond that 'inner circle' and has been regarded as including, the right to establish and develop relations with others in a business setting as well as other situations.

> **Case illustration**
>
> P was caught by CCTV in a high street with a knife in his hand after attempting to commit suicide. The CCTV operator notified the police who detained P under the Mental Health Act. He was examined and then released. The local authority used footage of this incident to publicise the effectiveness of the CCTV system. However, the footage did not suitably mask P's identity. The European Court held that even though he was in a public street, he was not there for a public event (such as a demonstration). He could be recognised by friends and family through the media images and so the exposure he received far exceeded that from a passer-by or from security observation. Therefore, it was found to be a violation of Article 8.[72]

8.90   There are a number of areas where the right to a private life exists. These include:

> - physical and moral integrity, for example not to be harassed or abused;
> - right to identity and personal development – sexual orientation;
> - gender identity, ie, transsexuals;
> - protection of reputation;
> - interception of communications and other types of surveillance;
> - personal data;
> - developing relations with others, both socially and in the work environment;
> - photographs, CCTV and video recordings;
> - environmental issues, such as noise pollution or toxic emissions.

Family life

8.91   Unlike the right to marry and found a family (article 12), the right to family life is not just concerned with the specific situations of being entitled to marry and have children. It is more generally concerned

72   *Peck v UK* (2003) 36 EHRR 41.

with what it means to be a family. Whether family life exists is affected, but not ultimately determined, by marriage-based relationships or biological ties. It is a question of fact dependent on evidence of close personal ties. The right to family life has been found in the following situations:

> • partners who are not married, so long as sufficient family ties exist, such as proof of the length of the relationship, having children together and financial ties;
> • relationships between gay or lesbian couples and transsexuals;
> • near relatives, such as grandparents and grandchildren;
> • relations between siblings;
> • relationships between uncles and aunts and nieces and nephews have also been included, although they may require greater proof;
> • adoption and fostering (such a placement does not necessarily extinguish all the rights of the natural parents).

Home

8.92   The concept of 'home' is another autonomous term that does not depend on any classification given by domestic law. It depends on certain factual issues, such as the existence of sufficient and continuous links with the property. The fact that a person unlawfully occupies a house or flat does not mean that the right to a home ceases to apply (although it is likely to be a significant factor when balancing the individual right with the interests of the community under article 8(2)).

8.93   The right to home includes the right to occupy an existing home without interference and to enjoy its comforts. Harassment by others and noise nuisance can violate this aspect, and in this situation, can apply to business as well as residential premises.

Correspondence

8.94   This covers all forms of communication such as telephone calls, facsimiles, letters, e-mail and text messages.

8.95   The right not to have correspondence interfered with may depend on certain factors. For example, the authorities will, in general, not be entitled to interfere with normal postal services. However, prisoners may be subject to greater interference, although correspondence with their lawyers cannot, in general, be interfered with.

8.96 The words 'respect for private and family life ... home and correspondence' means that the state does not only have a negative obligation not to interfere with these rights, but also positive obligations to respect them.[73]

Article 8(2)

8.97 Where it has been established that an article 8(1) right exists, it is necessary to see whether any interference to the right is justified in accordance with the limitations set out in article 8(2).[74]

8.98 The limitation must be in accordance with the law. It must also come within one of the specific list of legitimate aims set out in the Convention. These are:

- national security;
- public safety;
- the economic well-being of the country;
- the prevention of disorder or crime;
- the protection of health and morals;
- the protection of the rights and freedoms of others.

8.99 If it does come within one of the legitimate aims it must be necessary in a democratic society, proportionate and not discriminatory.

Article 9 – freedom of thought, conscience and religion

(1) Everyone has the right to freedom of thought, conscience and religion; this right includes freedom to change his religion or belief and freedom, either alone or in community with others and in public or private, to manifest his religion or belief, in worship, teaching, practice and observance.

73 See para 9.11.
74 See paras 10.19 – 10.26.

(2) Freedom to manifest one's religion or beliefs shall be subject only to such limitations as are prescribed by law and are necessary in a democratic society in the interests of public safety, for the protection of public order, health or morals, or for the protection of the rights and freedoms of others.

Article 9(1)

8.100   Article 9(1) can be broken down into two specific parts. The first is an unqualified right that protects a person's freedom of thought, conscience and religion. Freedom of religion includes freedom to change one's religion.

8.101   The second protects the freedom to carry out one's religion or belief. This is a qualified right. It covers a wide range of religions. However, this does not extend to purely idealistic or political beliefs.

8.102   The Strasbourg tribunal has sought to make a distinction when considering the manifestation of ones belief. Conduct that directly expresses a religion or belief is capable of being protected under article 9(1). Therefore, having a particular food diet (eg, kosher) is protected under article 9(1).[75] Conversely, conduct that is merely motivated by religion or belief is not protected. For instance, distributing pacifist literature or the non-payment of tax by Quakers where it was to be used on defence purposes.[76]

Article 9(2)

8.103   Where it has been established that an article 9(1) right exists, it is necessary to see whether any interference to the right is justified in accordance with the limitations set out in article 9(2).[77] The European Court has recognised that religious or philosophical convictions may polarise communities. It has stated that, 'Although it is possible that tension is created in situations where a religious or any other community becomes divided … this is one of the unavoidable consequences of pluralism. The role of the authorities in such circumstances is not to remove the cause of the tension by eliminating pluralism but to ensure that the competing groups tolerate each other.'[78]

---

75   *DS & ES v UK* (1990) 65 DR 245.
76   *C v UK* (1983) 37 DR 142.
77   See paras 10.19 – 10.26.
78   *Serif v Greece* (2001) 31 EHRR 20.

8.104   The limitation must be in accordance with the law. It must also come within one of the specific list of legitimate aims set out in the Convention. These are:

> - public safety;
> - the protection of health and morals;
> - the protection of the rights and freedoms of others.

8.105   If it does come within one of the legitimate aims it must be necessary in a democratic society, proportionate and non-discriminatory.

Article 10 – freedom of expression

(1) Everyone has the right to freedom of expression. This right shall include freedom to hold opinions and to receive and impart information and ideas without interference by public authority and regardless of frontiers. This article shall not prevent states from requiring the licensing of broadcasting, television or cinema enterprises.

(2) The exercise of these freedoms, since it carries with it duties and responsibilities, may be subject to such formalities, conditions, restrictions or penalties as are prescribed by law and are necessary in a democratic society, in the interests of national security, territorial integrity or public safety, for the prevention of disorder or crime, for the protection of health or morals, for the protection of the reputation or rights of others, for preventing the disclosure of information received in confidence, or for maintaining the authority and impartiality of the judiciary.

Article 10(1)

8.106 Freedom of expression is regarded as a cornerstone of democracy and a prerequisite for the enjoyment of many other rights. It entitles a person to hold opinions, and receive and impart information and ideas. It covers political speech, commercial speech and artistic expression, including pornography, offensive speech, protection of journalistic sources, licensing of broadcasting and television or cinema enterprises and access to information.

8.107   It should be noted that section 12 of the Human Rights Act 1998 seeks to enhance freedom of the press. This does not mean that freedom of expression will always prevail whenever it clashes with the right to privacy. However, where an interim injunction is sought to prevent publication, it should not be granted prior to a full hearing on the issue unless the court is satisfied that a full injunction is likely to be granted at the full hearing. The Court has confirmed that (i) there is no presumption that either Article 8 or Article 10 has, as such, precedence over the other; (ii) Where the values come in to conflict an intense focus on the comparative importance of the specific right being claimed will be required; (iii) the justification for interfering with each right must be taken into account; and (iv) the proportionality test must be applied when considering the limitations to each right.[79]

8.108   A restriction, other than a licensing restriction, will not violate article 10 if it is aimed at protecting one of the interests highlighted at para 8.110 below.

Article 10(2)

8.109   Where it has been established that an article 10(1) right exists, it is necessary to see whether any interference to the right is justified in accordance with the limitations set out in article 10(2).[80] It should be noted that article 10(2) makes reference to the 'duties and responsibilities' which accompany freedom of expression.

Case illustration

A prisoner who believed he had suffered a miscarriage of justice was denied the right to have an interview with journalists. It was highlighted that, 'The value of free speech must be considered in each particular case and that not every type of free speech has an equal value'. A comparison was made with the right of a prisoner to be granted an interview with journalists in order to discuss economic or political issues. In such a case it was believed that the prisoner's right to free speech could be justifiably limited because the person

---

79 *R v S (A Child)(Identification: Restrictions on Publication)* [2004] 3 WLR 1129.
80 See paras 10.19 – 10.26.

> had been deprived of their liberty as a result of being sentenced by the Court and because it was important for the authorities to have discipline and control in prisons. However, as it is assumed that every person has been correctly convicted, it was very important that a prisoner be allowed the right to speak to journalists in order to raise concerns about the safety of their conviction.[81]

8.110 The limitation must be in accordance with the law. It must also come within one of the specific list of legitimate aims set out in the Convention. These are:

> - national security;
> - territorial integrity or public safety;
> - the economic well-being of the country;
> - the prevention of disorder or crime;
> - the protection of health and morals;
> - the protection of the reputation and rights of others;
> - preventing the disclosure of information received in confidence;
> - maintaining the authority and impartiality of the judiciary.

8.111 If it does come within one of the legitimate aims it must be necessary in a democratic society, proportionate and non-discriminatory.

Article 11 – freedom of assembly and association

(1) *Everyone has the right to freedom of peaceful assembly and to freedom of association with others, including the right to form and to join trade unions for the protection of his interests.*

(2) *No restrictions shall be placed on the exercise of these rights other than such as are prescribed by law and are necessary in a*

---

81 The decision of Lord Steyn in *R v Secretary of State for the Home Department ex p Simms*, [2000] 2 AC 115.

democratic society in the interests of national security or public safety, for the prevention of disorder or crime, for the protection of health or morals or for the protection of the rights and freedoms of others. This article shall not prevent the imposition of lawful restrictions on the exercise of these rights by members of the armed forces, of the police or of the administration of the State.

Article 11(1)

8.112   Freedom of assembly includes marches as well as static assemblies and covers both public and private events. It confers a right to hold meetings, marches and demonstrations on the public highway.[82]

8.113   Freedom of association refers to the right of individuals to come together to further their common interests and, equally, includes the right not to belong to a trade union.[83] It does not include the right to share the company of others. Nor does it give a person the right to belong to a particular association.

8.114   Article 11 provides for the right to form and join trade unions. How much further this right extends to protecting trade union activity is unclear. The protection of trade union activity must be shown to be indispensable to the protection of its member's interests. It has been held that trade unions have a limited protection to be 'heard' in the collective bargaining process, but there is no general right to be consulted. Neither is the right to strike guaranteed.

Article 11(2)

8.115   Where it has been established that an article 11(1) right exists, it is necessary to see whether any interference to the right is justified in accordance with the limitations set out in article 11(2).[84]

8.116   Article 11(2) makes special reference to the military, police and civil service. This excludes them from much of the protection of article 11(2). Any interference with their article 11 rights will survive challenge so long as it is lawful.

8.117   The limitation must be in accordance with the law. It must also come within one of the specific list of legitimate aims set out in the Convention. These are:

82   *Jones & Lloyd v DPP* [1999] 2 AC 40.
83   *Young, James and Webster v UK* (1981) 4 EHRR 38.
84   See paras 10.19 – 10.26.

- national security;
- public safety;
- the prevention of disorder or crime;
- the protection of health and morals;
- the protection of the rights and freedoms of others.

8.118 If it does come within one of the legitimate aims it must be necessary in a democratic society, proportionate and non-discriminatory.

Article 12 – right to marry

Men and women of marriageable age have the right to marry and to found a family, according to the national laws governing the exercise of this right.

8.119 The right to marry has been interpreted as a legally binding association between a man and a woman. The scope of the right to marry is defined by the requirement that the couple be of marriageable age.

8.120 There is also an express limitation that the right to marry and found a family must comply with the rules of domestic law. This gives the authorities a certain amount of flexibility when placing limitations on this right, although, any limitation must not impair the very essence of the right and must be lawful and proportionate.[85]

Case illustration

A prisoner serving a life sentence who married a woman from the prison service asked for permission to artificially inseminate his wife. It was held that the restrictions found with respect to the right for family life under article 8(2),[86] equally applied to article 12 rights. The prisoner failed to establish in

85 See paras 10.13 – 10.26.
86 See paras 8.97 – 8.99.

> this case that the right to found a family extended to the right
> to do so by artificial insemination when justifiably excluded
> from the enjoyment of family life and conjugal rights.[87]

8.121   Preventing transsexuals from marrying in their new gender has now
been regarded as a violation under Article 12.[88]

Article 14 – prohibition of discrimination

*The enjoyment of the rights and freedoms set forth in this Convention
shall be secured without discrimination on any ground such as sex, race,
colour, language, religion, political or other opinion, national or social
origin, association with a national minority, property, birth or other
status.*

The meaning of discrimination

8.122   The list of discriminatory grounds is not exhaustively set out in the
Convention text, as highlighted by the words 'or other status' which
includes such elements as disability, conscientious objection,
illegitimacy and sexual orientation.

8.123   There are certain characteristics within the list that will require
very weighty reasons to be put forward before any differential
treatment is found to be justifiable. They relate to discrimination
based on sex, race, colour, nationality (but not with respect to
immigration), illegitimacy and religion.

When is differential treatment discriminatory?

8.124   Article 14 is not a freestanding right and can only be used in
conjunction with one of the other Convention rights.[89]

8.125   In order for treatment to be discriminatory, a person must be
treated less favourably than others in a similar or analogous position.

---

87   *R on the application of Mellor v Secretary of State for the home Department* [2001]
HRLR 783; (2001) 4 CCLR 71.

88   *Goodwin v UK* (2002) EHRR 447.

89   See paras 9.9 – 9.10.

For instance, one cannot make general comparisons between the rights of a prisoner and those of a person living within the community since they are not in similar or analogous situations.

8.126 Discrimination does not prohibit all types of distinction or differential treatment. When considering whether differential treatment is discriminatory one must ask:

Is there a reasonable and objective justification for the discrimination?

8.127 In order to determine this, it is necessary to ask the following two questions:

> - What is the aim of the measure?
> - Are the means employed and the aims sought to be realised proportionate?[90]

8.128 Differential treatment will not always be discriminatory if there is a reasonable or objective justification. This has been found in two types of situation: positive discrimination and indirect discrimination.

8.129 Discriminatory treatment will not necessarily violate article 14 if it treats a disadvantaged group differently in order to assist them in redressing an existing situation of inequality. The differential treatment must have a legitimate aim. This is known as positive discrimination.

> Therefore, the decision to justify tax legislation that gave married women who were sole breadwinners in the family greater tax incentives than men was found to be justifiable because it encouraged more women to work and would help to overcome male prejudices in the work place.[91]

8.130 Indirect discrimination occurs when members of a group are treated in the same way as other people, which does not take into account

90 See paras 10.19 – 10.26.
91 *Lindsay v UK* (1986) 49 DR 181.

the difference of their situation. Therefore, a violation will occur where public authorities fail to treat people differently without a reasonable and objective justification.

Case illustration

The Greek authorities disqualified a person from becoming a chartered accountant because he had a criminal record.
He had been convicted for refusing to wear military uniform, as it conflicted with his beliefs as a Jehovah's Witness.

The disqualification was found to be indirect discrimination because the Greek authorities did not discriminate in their rules between individuals who had committed felonies
(eg, fraud, assault, etc) and those who had criminal records because of their religious convictions that would not affect their suitability to enter into the profession.[92]

Article 1 of Protocol 1 – right to property

Every natural or legal person is entitled to the peaceful enjoyment of his possessions. No one shall be deprived of his possessions except in the public interest and subject to the conditions provided for by law and by the general principles of international law.

The preceding provisions shall not, however, in any way impair the right of a State to enforce such laws as it deems necessary to control the use of property in accordance with the general interest or to secure the payment of taxes or other contributions or penalties.

8.131　This guarantees the right to peaceful enjoyment of possessions. Possessions have been found to include:

- shares;
- patents;
- licenses (so long as they give rise to a reasonable and legitimate expectation of a lasting nature);
- restrictive covenants and receipt of rent on a property;

---

92 *Thlimmenos v Greece* (2001) 31 EHRR 411.

- leases;
- planning consents;
- the ownership of a debt (so long as it is sufficiently established);
- welfare benefits can also constitute possessions;
- goodwill.

8.132 There is no right to acquire possessions or property, but the right to exclude others from land is protected. The mere expectation that one will receive possessions is not protected.

8.133 However, public authorities may:
(a) deprive individuals of their possessions; and
(b) control the use of property subject to certain qualifications.

8.134 Deprivation refers to a permanent but not a temporary interference with property.

Deprivation is permitted only if it is:

(a) lawful;[93]
(b) in the public interest (such as the pursuit of social justice);
(c) in accordance with general principles of international law;
(d) reasonably proportionate (this is a 'fair balance' test which is less exacting than the proportionality test in the other qualified rights).

8.135 Any interference with the right to property must be proportionate. Unlike the test in the other qualified rights,[94] the Court has adopted the 'fair balance' test. The balance between the right of the individual and the public interest will not be achieved if the person deprived of their property has had to bear an excessive burden. In order to ensure reasonable proportionality is established procedural fairness may need to be introduced into any decision making process.[95]

---

93 See paras 10.13 – 10.18.
94 See paras 10.27 – 10.34.
95 *Sporrong and Lonroth v Sweden* (1983) 5 EHRR 35.

8.136   Control of property is permitted in a wide range of circumstances and reflects an assumption that some form of control over the enjoyment of possessions is inevitable in democratic societies. These include:

- requirements to use possessions or property in a particular way, for example, rent controls or planning controls;
- confiscation of assets in criminal proceedings;
- withdrawal of a licence;
- retroactive tax measures;
- refusal to register a person in a professional body.

The control of property must be:

(a) lawful;[96]
(b) in the public interest or aimed at securing the payment of taxes or other contributions or penalties; and
(c) deemed necessary by the state, ie, reasonably proportionate (this is a 'fair balance' test which is less exacting on public authorities than the proportionality test in the other qualified rights).

Article 2 of Protocol 1 – right not to be denied education

No person shall be denied the right to education. In the exercise of any functions which it assumes in relation to education and to teaching, the State shall respect the right of parents to ensure such education and teaching in conformity with their own religious and philosophical convictions.

8.137   The right is concerned with restricting state interference in education. It does not place a positive obligation on the state to meet the specific educational requests, such as the right of access to a particular school. This article focuses on the right of access to educational facilities that already exist.

8.138   The European Court has established an implied restriction to this right on the basis that state regulation is required as an integral

96   See paras 10.13 – 10.18.

aspect of the right to education. This regulation must not injure the substance of the right to education nor conflict with other Convention rights. Regulation can include compulsory schooling of persons before they reach a certain age coupled with the power to punish parents who refuse to comply with the requirements.

8.139 The right to respect for a parent's philosophical convictions in terms of education will be relevant so long as those convictions:

(a) are worthy of respect in a democratic society;

(b) are not incompatible with human dignity;

(c) do not conflict with the fundamental right of the child to education.

Case illustration

Parents of children with special needs have the right to advance that the needs of their child require special facilities that may have to be respected by the educational authorities. However, this is not an absolute right, and authorities will have discretion as to how they allocate limited resources. Authorities can legitimately seek to integrate a child with special needs into mainstream schools even if this is not what parents may want.[97]

8.140 Provided an objective standard is met, state and private schools can teach material that conflicts with the religious or philosophical beliefs of a child's parents.

8.141 The UK has made a reservation to part of this right.[98]

Article 3 of Protocol 1 – the right to free elections

The High Contracting Parties undertake to hold free elections at reasonable intervals by secret ballot, under conditions which will ensure the free expression of the opinion of the people in the choice of the legislature.

8.142 Free elections place positive obligations on states. The protection concerns the right to vote and to stand for election. Although this is

---

97 *Simpson v UK* (1989) 64 DR 188.
98 See para 9.32.

an unqualified right, it is subject to an implied restriction, since it is accepted that countries may adopt laws that restrict who can vote or stand for election, so long as these restrictions are lawful and proportionate.

8.143　　The right contained in this article only relates to parliamentary elections and not local elections or national referenda. Nor does it oblige countries to introduce any particular system of election.

8.144　　Restrictions on electoral campaigning, such as electoral expenditure, may raise issues. Where statutory limits on election expenditure is operated as a total barrier to the applicant's ability to publish information with a view to influencing voters, the aim of the provision, ie, to secure equality between the candidates, is legitimate but the restriction is disproportionate.[99]

Article 1 of Protocol 6 – abolition of the death penalty

The death penalty shall be abolished. No one shall be condemned to such penalty or executed.

8.145　This abolishes capital punishment during peace time.

Article 2 of Protocol 6 – death penalty in the time of war

A state may make provision in its law for the death penalty in respect of acts committed in time of war or of imminent threat of war; such penalty shall be applied only in the instances laid down in the law and in accordance with its provisions. The State shall communicate to the Secretary General of the Council of Europe the relevant provisions of that law.

8.146　This states that the UK may make provision for the death penalty in times of war or where there is an imminent threat of war. This law cannot be made retrospectively and will need to have been firstly placed before the Secretary General of the Council of Europe.

99 *Bowman v UK* (1998) 26 EHRR 1.

CHAPTER 9

Understanding the Convention rights

Introduction

9.1   The articles contained in the European Convention are made up of rights and duties. On the one hand, rights tell individuals of the fundamental protection to which they are entitled. On the other, duties tell states what they must do, refrain from doing or ensure that individuals refrain from doing in order to ensure that those rights are protected. It is only when these two elements are put together that the Convention articles can be properly understood. Rights differ in their scope and the level of protection they provide for an individual. Duties differ in the extent of the obligation that they place on public authorities.

9.2   In order to understand the different rights and duties that are included in the Convention, this chapter is divided into four sections. The first section will show the different classifications that divide all the rights contained in the European Convention and those Optional Protocols signed by the UK. The second section will take a specific look at the different rights included in the Convention. The third section will examine the different types of duties placed on those with responsibility for the protection of rights. The final section will look at other articles contained in the European Convention, which might need to be considered when determining the extent to which rights may be restricted.

Different classifications of rights

9.3   The rights contained in the European Convention can be divided into four general categories:

- absolute rights;
- unqualified rights;
- qualified rights and
- conjunctive rights.

9.4   The general rule is that it is possible to divide these rights up into the different groups by asking the following two questions:[1]

(a) will a public authority be allowed to depart from its obligations to protect the right in question in the event of war or a period of

---

1   Conjunctive rights are a special case and will require different questions to be asked.

national emergency (such a restriction is called a derogation and is defined below);[2] and

(b) does the Convention right state that it can be balanced with the needs of other individuals or any general public interest?

Absolute rights

- the right to life (article 2);
- freedom from torture, cruel, inhuman and degrading treatment or punishment (article 3);
- freedom from slavery or servitude (article 4(1));
- the prohibition of retrospective criminal penalties (article 7).

9.5 Public authorities cannot depart from their obligations established under an absolute right during war or a period of national emergency. Nor can an absolute right be balanced against the needs of other individuals or the public interest, except in rare circumstances where two absolute rights are to be balanced against each other.

Unqualified rights

- freedom from forced labour (articles 4(2) and (3));
- the right to liberty and security of the person (article 5);
- the right to a fair trial (article 6);
- freedom of thought and conscience, and the right to believe in or change religion (article 9(1)) (this does not include freedom to manifest religion which is a qualified right see below);
- the right to marry and found a family (article 12);
- the right to not be denied education (article 2 of protocol 1);
- the right to free elections (article 3 of protocol 1);
- the abolition of the death penalty (articles 1 and 2 of the sixth protocol).

---

2 See para 9.33.

9.6   These are similar to absolute rights. They cannot be balanced against the needs of other individuals or against any general public interest. However, a public authority may be allowed to depart from its obligations in times of war or national emergency, so long as derogation has been made.[3]

> Article 5 establishes that there are only limited situations where a person may be lawfully deprived of their liberty.
> These are set out in article 5(1)(a) – (f).

Qualified rights

> * the right to respect for private and family life, home and correspondence (article 8);
> * freedom to manifest ones religion (article 9);
> * freedom of expression (article 10);
> * freedom of assembly and association (article 11);
> * the right to property (article 1 of protocol 1).

9.7   These are rights which can not only be departed from in times of war or national emergency, (so long as a derogation has been made)[4] but may also be interfered with in order to protect the rights of another or the wider public interest.

9.8   In general, qualified rights are structured so that the first part of the article sets out the right that is to be protected, while the second part establishes whether a public authority can legitimately interfere with that right in order to protect the wider public interest.[5]

---

3   For the definition of 'derogation' see para 9.33.
4   Ibid.
5   See articles 8(2), 9(2), 10(2) and 11(2) in chapter 8. A different test is applied for the right to property in article 1 of protocol 1, see para 8.135.

Conjunctive rights

> The prohibition on discrimination (article 14).

9.9 What makes a conjunctive right different from all the other types of rights is that it is not freestanding. This means that a claim can only be made in conjunction with one of the other types of Convention right (ie, absolute, qualified or unqualified rights).[6]

> **Case illustration**
>
> Where a child was only entitled to inherit a smaller share of her mother's estate simply because she had been born outside of marriage, the European Court found that the right to property (article 1 of protocol 1) was applicable. Therefore, the discriminatory treatment of the child born outside of marriage could be brought in relation to that right.[7]

9.10 As long as the claim legitimately raises an issue under one of the other Convention rights, the fact that no violation of that other Convention right is found does not mean that the conjunctive right will also fail.

> **Case illustration**
>
> For instance, a woman who was permanently resident in the UK complained that her right to family life under article 8 was interfered with because her foreign husband was not entitled to join her. The policy of the UK to restrict admission of non-national spouses into the UK was regarded as justifiable, and so did not contravene article 8. However, the fact that the

---

6 Protocol 12 to the European Convention would make the prohibition of discrimination 'on any grounds such as sex, race, colour, language, religion, political or other opinion, national or social origin, association with a national minority, property, birth or other status' a freestanding right. However, the UK has not signed this protocol yet.

7 *Marckx v Belgium* (1980) 2 EHRR 330.

> policy allowed non-national females to be permitted entry into
> the UK and not non-national males was discriminatory and,
> therefore, a violation of article 14.[8]

The different rights contained in the Convention

9.11   Not all rights and restrictions are expressly set out in the text of the
Convention. There are specific rights and restrictions that are not
included within the Convention articles but have been established by
the European Court in order to ensure the effective application of the
Convention right in question. These are known as implied rights or
restrictions.

9.12   It should be emphasised, that these implied rights and
restrictions do not create new human rights; they simply ensure that
the Convention article in question can be applied in a practical and
effective manner.[9] They are present in only a limited number of
rights.

Implied rights found in the Convention
- The right of access to Court and the right to adequate
  participation have been implied into article 6(1).[10]

Implied restrictions found in the Convention
- The right not to be denied education (article 2 of
  protocol 1).[11]
- The right to free elections (article 3 of protocol 1).[12]
- The right to cross-examine witnesses in criminal
  proceedings is restricted (article 6(3)(d)).[13]

---

8   *Abdulaziz, Cabales and Balkandali v UK* (1985) 7 EHRR 471.
9   This ensures that Convention rights are secured in accordance with article 1 of
the Convention, and is in accordance with the principle that rights must be
applicable in practice and not just in theory. See para 10.8.
10   See para 8.76.
11   See para 8.138.
12   See para 8.142.
13   See para 8.85.

The scope of the rights

9.13 There are four questions that should be considered in order to understand the scope of a right:

(1) What rights does the particular article of the Convention say it protects?

9.14 It is not difficult to recognise the general right that each Convention provision aims to protect.

> For example, article 2(1) states that UK law must protect everyone's right to life.

(2) Does the article of the Convention place any restrictions on these rights?

9.15 The Convention recognises that there are occasions where rights will need to be limited in order to protect the rights of another person or the public interest.

> For example, it is clearly the case that the right of a person not to be deprived of their liberty under article 5 can be limited in order to protect other members of society from serious criminal acts.

(3) Are there any rights not contained in the article of the Convention (ie, implied rights) that must be included in order for the right to be properly effective?

> The European Court has implied into the article 6 right to a fair trial that parties must have the 'right to participate effectively' in any civil proceedings, even though this is not explicitly mentioned in the text.[14]

14 See at para 8.76.

(4)   Are there any restrictions that are not contained in the article of the Convention (ie, implied restrictions) that must be included in order for the right to be properly effective?

> The European Court has accepted that the right to hold free elections (article 3 of protocol 1) can be subject to implied limitations that allow national authorities to regulate the right to vote or to stand for election in certain limited situations. These may, for example, allow states to prevent children, mental health patients or prisoners from voting or standing for election.[15] Human rights principles ensure that these implied restrictions are lawful and proportionate to their aim.[16]

What duties do public authorities have to protect rights?

9.16   The European Convention places two types of obligation on states in the protection of the rights of their citizens, negative and positive obligations.[17]

Negative obligations

9.17   This places a duty on the state to refrain from acting in a way that interferes with a person's Convention rights.

---

15 *R on the application of Pearson v Secretary of State for the Home Department* [2001] HRLR 806.

16 See paras 10.13 – 10.26.

17 Although the Human Rights Act is directly concerned with the duties of public authorities, this does not mean that private individuals do not have some responsibility for their treatment of each other under the European Convention. There are two particular ways in which the European Convention indirectly relates to private individuals. Firstly, positive obligations on public authorities (see below) mean that they can be liable for not effectively protecting the Convention rights of one private individual from another. The second stems from the inclusion of courts and tribunals in the list of public authorities (see section 6(3)(a) of the Human Rights Act 1998). As a result, courts and tribunals have a duty to protect Convention rights even if the parties before them are both private individuals.

> For instance, the article 3 right puts a duty on the state not to subject a person to any treatment or punishment that would be regarded as torture, inhuman or degrading.

9.18 The straightforward question to be asked in order to determine the negative obligations on state authorities is:

Has the public authority carried out an act which interferes with a person's Convention right?

If the answer to the first question is 'yes', the following question must be asked:

Does the Convention entitle the public authority to carry out that act under the Convention?

For instance, the right to protest under article 9(1) may be interfered with under article 9(2) where it is lawful, has a legitimate aim and is necessary in a democratic society.[18]

Positive obligations

9.19 Positive obligations place a duty on state authorities to take active steps in order to safeguard a person's Convention rights.

9.20 Unlike negative obligations, most positive obligations are not included in the text of the Convention. There are exceptions, such as the duty to create laws to protect the right to life under article 2(1) and the duty to respect the right to private and family life, home and correspondence under article 8. The majority of positive obligations have been read into the Convention in order to ensure that the fundamental rights contained in the Convention are respected. This is in accordance with article 1 of the European Convention which calls on states to secure all the rights and freedoms contained in the Convention, article 13 which establishes the right to an effective

18 See paras 8.103 – 8.105.

remedy, and one of the Convention principles, that rights should be practical and effective and not theoretical and illusory.[19]

9.21   The European Court has not been prepared to set out the principles behind its use of positive obligations. However, it is possible to establish five different types of positive obligation from the Strasbourg case law which state authorities may be under a duty to protect.

> (a) The duty to provide resources to individuals in order to protect a Convention right.
> (b) The duty to put in place a legal framework which provides effective protection of Convention rights.
> (c) The duty to prevent breaches of Convention rights.
> (d) The duty to provide information to those whose Convention rights are at risk.
> (e) The duty to respond to breaches of Convention rights.

(a)   The duty to provide resources to individuals in order to protect a Convention right.

9.22   The onus on public authorities to provide these resources may be significant. In many situations the obligation is easily recognisable. States will need to commit considerable resources if they are to meet their obligations to provide education (article 2 of protocol 1) or free and fair political elections (article 3 of protocol 1). However, the duty to provide resources is not always so obvious.

> The failure of the police to provide resources to effectively protect the right of peaceful assembly resulted in a violation of article 11. The European Court found that preventative injunctions given by the authorities were of limited use if they were not enforced by the police.[20]

---

19 See paras 10.8 – 10.10.
20 *Plattform Artze fur das Leben v Austria* (1991) 13 EHRR 204.

(b)   The duty to put in place a legal framework which provides effective protection of Convention rights

9.23   The government has responsibility for establishing legislation which ensures that the Convention rights of a private individual or body will not be breached by another.

> The failure to adequately provide legislation which prevented a stepfather beating his child with a garden rake was found to violate article 3.[21]

(c)   The duty to prevent breaches of Convention rights

9.24   Public authorities have a duty to take operational measures, which are within their powers to protect individuals who face risks to their well-being.

> A local authority had a duty to separate four children from their mother as it had clear information that the children were being subjected to considerable abuse and neglect while in her care.[22]

(d)   A duty to provide information to those whose Convention rights are at risk

9.25   Where a state engages in or allows private bodies to carry out hazardous activities, it must provide individuals with an accessible procedure which allows them to obtain all relevant and appropriate information.

> An authority became aware that a neighbourhood was facing a strong risk of pollution from a private waste treatment factory nearby. Although, the authority was not responsible for the risk of pollution, it failed to provide the information to those affected by it, including what to do in the event of an accident. The Court found the authorities to be in breach of the right to privacy, family life and home under article 8.[23]

21 *A v UK* (1998) 27 EHRR 611.
22 *Z v UK* (2002) 34 EHRR 97.
23 *Guerra v Italy* (1998) 26 EHRR 357.

(e)   A duty to respond to breaches of Convention rights

9.26   Where the authorities are informed that a Convention right has been breached, there is a duty to carry out efficient and thorough investigations.

> Where a prisoner died of a severe asthma attack, there was a duty to carry out a full, effective and impartial investigation, which includes ensuring that witnesses give testimony.[24]

9.27   When considering whether public authorities are under a positive obligation to protect a Convention right, two questions need to be considered:

(1)   What positive steps are required of the public authority to protect the Convention right?

9.28   This should come within one of the duties set out in (a) to (e) above.

(2)   What steps must those with responsibility take in order to discharge their positive obligations?

9.29   While public authorities are under a duty to prevent or investigate breaches, it would be unfair to place unrealistic or impossible burdens on them to protect Convention rights. The duty on public authorities only extends to protecting a real and immediate risk to a Convention right that they are reasonably expected to foresee and prevent. These limitations on the positive duties are partly designed to take into account resource limitations and the extent of the knowledge before them. Further, public authorities must be aware that the presumptuous detention of a person may result in a violation of that person's right not to be deprived of their liberty (article 5) or their private life (article 8).

---

24   *R on the application of Margaret Wright v Secretary of State for the Home Department* (2002) HRLR 1.

Case illustration

A case was brought against the police for not taking positive steps to prevent a person from killing someone, even though the police had been made aware of the person's unhealthy fascination with the dead man and his family. The Court recognised that the right to life implied that state authorities owe individuals a positive duty to take operational measures to protect an individual whose life is at risk from the criminal acts of another person. However, the Court also recognised that such an obligation could not place an impossible or disproportionate burden on the police, and that not every claimed threat to life created such a positive obligation.

The police must have failed to take measures within the scope of their powers which, judged reasonably might have been expected to avoid that risk. Account needed to be taken of the difficulties of policing in a modern society.

This includes difficult choices which the police may have to make with respect to their priorities and the use of their resources. Furthermore, the presumptuous detention of a person without strong enough evidence may result in that person claiming a deprivation of their liberty under article 5. The court established that there must be a real and immediate risk to life about which the authorities knew or ought to have known before they were under a positive duty to intervene.[25]

Other types of restriction found in the European Convention on Human Rights

Restrictions contained in articles 16 and 17

9.30 Article 16 states that nothing in the right to freedom of expression (article 10), freedom of association and assembly (article 11) or the prohibition on discrimination (article 14) will be able to prevent the authorities from restricting the political activities of aliens (ie, individuals from another country that do not have residence in the

25 *Osman v UK* (1998) 29 EHRR 245.

UK). This provision is to be narrowly interpreted since the Convention rights are evolving and developing and must be considered in the light of present day conditions.[26]

9.31   Article 17 restricts any person who is trying to perform an act aimed at destroying other Convention rights. Any restriction must be limited in its scope and duration so that it is strictly proportionate to the threat to another's Convention rights. It is aimed at extremists who seek to use the Convention rights to promote acts that will destroy the Convention rights of others.

> Article 17 may be used to justify the exclusion of a candidate whose election leaflets are likely to incite racial hatred.[27]

Reservations

9.32   When signing up to the Convention or an Optional Protocol, states can enter reservations with the Council of Europe which recognise that they are not yet in a position to protect a particular right, and as such should not be found to have violated that right until they decide to remove the reservation. Reservations are seen as undesirable and will not be automatically accepted by the European Court. Objections can be made by the Court or another country if the language of the reservation is too wide or vague, or if it conflicts with the object and purpose of the Convention.[28] Reservations are referred to in section 15 and schedule 3 of the Human Rights Act 1998.

> The UK has made a reservation with respect to the second paragraph of the right to education (article 2 of protocol 1). It states that, in relation to education and teaching, a parent will have the right to ensure that their child's education is provided in conformity with their own religious and philosophical convictions only to the extent that it is compatible with the provision of efficient instruction and training and the avoidance of unreasonable public expenditure.

26 See paras 10.8 – 10.10.
27 *Kuhnen v Germany* (1988) 56 DR 205.
28 See para 10.4.

Derogations

9.33 There are some situations where a state is entitled to restrict, or in other words, derogate from its obligations under the Convention. A derogation will only be acceptable if it is made for a legitimate and justifiable purpose. It can only be made in a time of war or public emergency threatening the life of the nation, where the circumstances make it strictly necessary. Derogations will not be acceptable if they are too broad or vague. A country is not allowed to derogate against an absolute right.[29] Sections 14 and 16 of the Human Rights Act 1998 state that derogation can be made by the Secretary of State. It will be effective for up to five years unless it is renewed.

Case illustration

Following the terrorist attacks in New York, Washington and Pennsylvania on September 11, 2001, the UK government submitted a derogation to article 5(1)(f). Prior to the derogation a person could not be detained in the UK under article 5(1)(f) if it was not going to be possible to deport or extradite them.[30] One such situation would be where the person faced a real risk of serious or irreparable harm if sent to the receiving country. This meant it would not be possible for the UK authorities to deport or extradite a person to the USA if they were likely to face inhuman and degrading treatment or punishment in breach of article 3 when on death row. Accordingly, the person could not then be detained in the UK under article 5(1)(f). As a result, the government submitted a derogation after September 11 allowing the UK authorities to continue to detain terrorist suspects who cannot be deported or extradited because they will be at risk of serious or irreparable harm from the receiving country.[31]

---

29 See para 9.5.
30 See para 8.38.
31 However, this policy was successfully challenged in the courts (see *A v Secretary of State for the Home Department* referred to in para 7.21 above). This led to the drawing up of 'control orders' which have also been the subject of successful challenge in the Courts. See *Secretary of State for the Home Department v JJ and others* [2007] UKHL 45.

CHAPTER 10

Human rights principles in the European Convention on Human Rights

Introduction

10.1 The European Convention on Human Rights is an international human rights treaty. As such, it is underpinned by certain basic principles of interpretation, which are established through rules of international law.[1] This chapter will firstly look at the principles of interpretation which apply to the European Convention. It will then consider principles that have been established by the European Court of Human Rights, focusing on the extent to which states can restrict or interfere with a human right established under the Convention.

10.2 The European Convention has the most developed case law of any regional or international human rights treaty. This is because the European Court has been established longer and taken considerably more cases than any other international human rights tribunal. While the European Court has occasionally considered rights included in other international human rights treaties to assist in its decision-making,[2] it seeks to interpret the human rights contained in the Convention in a manner that reflects the cultural standards and values regarded as common to Europe.

Principles of interpretation under international law

10.3 A key principle of international law is to recognise the 'object and purpose' of an international treaty. For instance, where two countries enter into an international agreement on a particular matter, it will often be quite easy to understand the intention of the parties by examining the terms of the treaty. However, international human rights law is more complex. Firstly, not all countries that are now a party to the Convention were involved in its drafting. Secondly, the Convention is not just supposed to reflect the values of society at the time the treaty was drafted. Standards required for the protection of fundamental rights continue to grow as the fundamental values of democratic societies develop.

---

1 These principles have been set out in an international law treaty, the Vienna Convention on the Law of Treaties 1969.

2 See para 7.25.

The object and purpose of the European Convention

10.4   The object and purpose of the European Convention on Human Rights is to ensure:

(a)   the maintenance, realisation and protection of human rights; and

(b)   the protection and promotion of the ideas and values that lie at the heart of a democratic society. These have been referred to as the concepts of 'pluralism, tolerance and broad-mindedness'.

10.5   The European Court has recognised that Convention rights are supposed to be given a wide rather than a restrictive interpretation. Therefore, when considering whether or not a Convention right applies, decision-makers should not be thinking 'how best can I limit the application of a Convention right'? Instead, it is important to ask the question: 'Do my actions realise the aims and objectives of the European Convention on Human Rights?'

10.6   The following principles have been established in order to give effect to the object and purpose of the Convention.

Rights have an independent meaning

10.7   The European Court will not necessarily accept the definition given to words and phrases contained in the Convention by national authorities. The effectiveness of the Convention could be undermined if countries were able to establish their own meanings for key words contained in Convention rights.[3] The independent meaning of words also allows for greater consistency in the application of rights among states that are party to the Convention.

Rights must be practical and effective

10.8   The safeguards required to protect human rights must not only be available in theory, but be practical and effective. This means that public authorities cannot simply put forward vague or abstract measures to protect rights that will have no practical effect.

10.9   The need to ensure that Convention rights are practically effective has led to the imposition of positive obligations and implied rights by the European Court.[4]

---

3   See, for example, the process by which the court established the meaning of the right to home in *Harrow LBC v Qazi* (2002) UKHRR 316.

4   See chapter 9.

Rights are evolving and developing

10.10 The provisions of the European Convention are not crystallised in time to the period when they were drafted. They must be considered in the light of present day conditions. As such, the European Convention is referred to as a 'living instrument'. Standards may be raised as a result of scientific developments, psychological research, social progression or changes in moral attitudes. The Strasbourg case law has sometimes reflected these changes before national laws.

> **Case illustration**
>
> A post-operative male to female transsexual complained about the failure of the authorities to change her name and birth records which listed her as 'male'. The European Court had previously accepted the UK's justifications for interfering with the right to private and family life. However, it recognised the problems facing transsexuals and stressed the need for legal measures in this area to be kept under review. The Court found that the traditional arguments of the UK were no longer sustainable, and found there to be a violation under article 8.[5]

Principles established by the European Court of Human Rights

10.11 While public authorities must give Convention rights a wide interpretation, restrictions and interferences to a right must be narrowly defined. This section will first set out the different types of restriction or interference which are placed on Convention rights. It will then consider principles that have been established by the European Court to ensure that restrictions do not reach beyond their purpose.

> • Restrictions may be expressly provided for in the Convention articles. See, for example, article 2(2), article 5(1)(a) – (f) and article 12.

5 *Goodwin v UK* (2002) 35 EHRR 447.

> - Rights which are implied into the Convention also contain restrictions. For example, the European Court has established that the civil fair trial right of access to court which has been implied into article 6(1) does not provide for access in every situation.[6]
> - Interferences with a qualified or conjunctive right may be justifiable. See articles 8(2), 9(2), 10(2), 11(2), article 1 of protocol 1 and article 14.
> - Restrictions of qualified and unqualified rights can be made through a valid derogation.

10.12   There are four particular areas to consider when examining the legitimacy of the restriction to a Convention right. The two principles of 'legality' and 'proportionality' are to be applied to every restriction. The justification for an interference relates to qualified or conjunctive rights. Finally, it is necessary to consider the impact of the discretion which public authorities are given when carrying out their functions and the approach to blanket policies and immunities.

The principle of legality

10.13   The principle of legality is referred to in several Convention rights. As well as using the term 'lawful', the European Convention also refers to the terms 'prescribed by law' and 'in accordance with the law'. These terms all have the same meaning. The principle of legality is not only concerned with the domestic law. It also incorporates what is known as the rule of law. This means that any action by public authorities which interferes with a Convention right must provide a certain measure of protection from arbitrariness. This may be particularly relevant where the interference does not have a basis in law, or where the powers given to public authorities are very broad or vague.

6   See para 8.78.

Convention rights that refer to the lawfulness of restrictions

Article 5(1)
Article 8(2)
Article 9(2)
Article 10(2)
Article 11(2)
Article 12
Article 1 of Protocol 1
Article 1 of Protocol 1
Article 2 of Protocol 6

10.14 In order to establish the lawfulness of a restriction the European Court will ask the following three questions:

- Is the law identified and established in the UK?
- Is the law adequately accessible?
- Is the law sufficiently foreseeable?

The first is based on the subjective identification of a law by the national authorities. The Court adopts an objective approach when asking the final two questions.

The law must be identified and established in domestic law

10.15 Domestic law can mean the following:
(a) primary legislation;
(b) secondary legislation;
(c) common law;
(d) European Community law;
(e) The rules of professional bodies, such as medical and legal bodies, so long as the rules are available to those who are bound by them.

Is the law publicly accessible?

10.16 Individuals must be able to find out about the legal requirements that are placed upon them. Therefore, they must be published in a form that is publicly accessible to those likely to be affected. For instance, Home Office guidelines, internal police guidelines or prison instructions which are neither published nor made accessible to the public will not satisfy this requirement.[7] The fact that a person has to consult a lawyer for effective access to the law in question does not of itself mean that the law has not been made sufficiently accessible.[8]

Is the law sufficiently precise for a person to be able to regulate their behaviour accordingly?

10.17 An individual who is capable of being affected by a law must be able to understand the circumstances in which it might be imposed in order that they may be able to foresee the consequences of any intended action with a certain degree of accuracy.

Case illustration

In the case of telephone tapping, the European Court found that there was a violation of the right to private life if the law did not establish the categories of people liable to have their phones tapped or the categories of offences for which tapping was authorised. The European Court also found that the failure to have limits on the duration of a telephone tap, the lack of rules on the disclosure of records created by the tapping and the failure to create rules governing the disposal of information following the acquittal or discontinuance of a case violated article 8.[9]

10.18 While a person should be able to recognise the consequences of their actions, absolute certainty is not required in order for a provision to be foreseeable as this would lead to excessive rigidity that might prevent the law from keeping pace with changing social circumstances. The fact that a statutory provision is capable of more than one interpretation will not necessarily mean that it is uncertain. Nor will changes to a common law offence over a period of time mean that it is uncertain provided that they are foreseeable and consistent with the essence of the offence.[10] The fact that a person

---

7 *Silver v UK* (1983) 5 EHRR 347.
8 *Sunday Times v UK* (1979) 2 EHRR 245.
9 *Malone v UK* (1984) 7 EHRR 14.
10 *SW and CR v UK* (1995) 21 EHRR 363.

has to consult a lawyer for effective access to the law in question does not of itself mean that the law has not been made sufficiently accessible.[11]

The principle of proportionality

10.19 Although the term 'proportionality' does not appear in the Convention it is regarded as a defining characteristic in the approach to the protection of human rights. It has been said to run like a golden thread through the Convention case law. In order for a restriction to be proportionate, a decision-maker must find a 'fair balance' between the protection of an individual right and the interests of the community at large.[12] Therefore, a restriction will only be proportionate if it does not go beyond the legitimate aim that it seeks to achieve.

Situations where the principle of proportionality is required

- To determine whether an interference with a qualified or conjunctive right is 'necessary'.
- To consider whether a restriction to an absolute right is strictly necessary.[13]
- To determine whether an implied restriction only meets the aim it seeks to achieve.
- To determine whether a derogation is sufficiently narrow so as to be acceptable.

10.20 In many cases it will be obvious whether a restriction or interference with a right is a proportionate response. However, it may prove useful to ask the following five questions to determine whether a restrictive act is proportionate or not.

Does a less restrictive alternative exist?

10.21 The restriction is unlikely to be proportionate where an equally effective yet less restrictive action can be taken in order to achieve the objective.

11 *Sunday Times v UK* (1979) 2 EHRR 245.
12 *Soering v UK* (1989) 11 EHRR 439.
13 See para 8.8 for the example of *McCann v UK* with respect to the use of lethal force by the authorities.

Case illustration

A blanket policy was established to allow prison officers to search the correspondence of prisoners without them being present for security purposes. While the prisoners did not claim that legal correspondence should be immune from such examination, they argued that the search should take place in their presence. They feared that prison officers might do more than just briefly examine the legal documents and this may inhibit the willingness of prisoners to communicate freely with legal advisers. The prison services claimed that if prisoners were present, they might intimidate staff or disrupt the search. The courts held that prisoners could be excluded in those situations, but that the blanket policy preventing prisoners from being present was disproportionate as a less restrictive, but equally effective alternative existed.[14]

Are the reasons for the restriction 'relevant and sufficient'?

10.22   It is not enough that the decision is made carefully and in good faith; the reasons advanced must be relevant and sufficient to the aim sought.

Case illustration

In the UK age of consent for sex was higher for homosexuals than heterosexuals, the European Court found that, although government concern that a lowering of the age would erode existing moral standards was relevant, it was not sufficient to justify criminalising homosexual relations between those capable of valid consent.[15]

---

14   *R v Secretary of State for the Home Department ex p Daly* [2001] 1 WLR 2099.
15   *Dudgeon v UK* (1982) 4 EHRR 149.

Has sufficient regard been paid to the rights and interests of those affected?

10.24 In situations where a Convention right is restricted by public authorities exercising their discretion, a fair procedure must be established to ensure that due respect is afforded to the right that is being restricted. Such fairness may be required for administrative decisions that would not be covered under article 6 fair trial rights. These have been found to be relevant in right to family life and right to property.

Case illustration

The failure to allow a parent to be involved in the decision making process concerning their separation from their children while in care, was in breach of the article 8 right to family life.[16]

Case illustration

A couple complained about their inability to see confidential reports that had been relied upon in the decision to take their child into care even though no special reasons for withholding the report had been advanced. The Court held that the non-disclosure did not afford requisite protection of their article 8 rights.[17]

Do safeguards exist against error or abuse?

10.25 Any interference by public authorities must be subject to an effective control which should be assured by a judicial body which is independent and impartial.

---

16 *Olsson v Sweden (No 1)* (1988) 11 EHRR 259.
17 *McMichael v UK* (1995) 20 EHRR 205.

> The practice of telephone tapping as a form of secret surveillance was not proportionate where there was no judicial control offering best guarantees of independence, impartiality and proper procedure.[18]

Does the restriction in question destroy the very essence of the Convention right at issue?

10.26   This is particularly relevant in situations where decision-makers are given considerable discretion to determine when a right should be restricted.

> **Case illustration**
>
> The decision to place a temporary prohibition on a man remarrying after three divorces in quick succession affected the very essence of the right to marry and was regarded as being disproportionate to the aim of achieving stability in marriage.[19]

The justification for interference to a qualified right

10.27   This section is concerned with the test to determine whether interferences to articles 8 to 11 will be justifiable. The process for determining whether the interference to a property right under article 1 of protocol 1 or a discriminatory measure under article 14 is justifiable has been set out in a previous chapter.[20] The following consideration will need to be given to every decision that affects a right contained in articles 8 to 11.

Is the restriction in accordance with the law?

10.28   In the first place, any restriction to the rights contained in these articles must be in accordance with the law.[21]

---

18   *Klass v Germany* (1980) 2 EHRR 214.
19   *F v Switzerland* (1988) 10 EHRR 411.
20   See chapter 8.
21   See paras 10.13 – 10.18.

Does it have a legitimate aim?

10.29 They must meet one of the legitimate aims set out in the provision. Public authorities may only rely on the expressly stated legitimate aims when restricting the right in question. There is no entitlement to introduce any other legitimate aims in order to justify interfering with a qualified right.

10.30 The legitimate aims contained in qualified rights vary, but are in general used to protect one of the following interests:
(a) national security;
(b) public safety;
(c) the protection of health and morals;
(d) the prevention of crime and disorder;
(e) the protection of the rights of others.

Is the restriction necessary in a democratic society?

10.31 The European Court has established that the word 'necessary' does not mean 'indispensable' or 'reasonable'. It has stated that 'necessary' implies the existence of a 'pressing social need'. This can be taken to mean that public authorities will need to demonstrate that there is a need for the restriction.

Case illustration

The decision to obtain an injunction preventing the publication of the Spycatcher book, written by a former security services agent for security reasons, served a legitimate aim, but was no longer necessary in a democratic society once the book was in the public domain.[22]

10.32 The term in 'a democratic society' does not mean that the will of the majority shall always prevail. Ideas that shock or offend are still to be protected.

---

22 *The Observer and The Guardian v UK* (1992) 14 EHRR 153.

Case illustration

The European Court found that, while members of the public who saw homosexuality as immoral and may be shocked by the idea of homosexual acts taking place, this did not warrant criminal sanctions against consenting adults who engaged in private homosexual acts.[23]

Proportionality

10.33   Although, it is not set out in the Convention, the principle of proportionality is closely linked with the term 'necessary' since a restriction cannot be necessary unless it is proportionate to the legitimate aim pursued. Therefore, it will be necessary to ensure that any decision fairly balances the rights of the individual with those of the wider public interest.

Discrimination

10.34   Having determined whether the interference with one of the article 8 to 11 rights is in accordance with the law, has a legitimate aim, is necessary in a democratic society and proportionate, the Court must finally ensure that it is not discriminatory.

Discretion and immunities

The need for a 'margin of discretion' under the Human Rights Act 1998

10.36   The courts have recognised the need to give public authorities a margin of discretion in their decision making. This reflects the possibility that they may have to deal with sensitive issues in which the decisions of the legislative, executive or other public bodies have wider policy implications.

10.37   This is slightly different from a similar term, the 'margin of appreciation'. This term from international law, is used by the European Court to explain the latitude that may be given to individual countries when the European Court makes decisions.

---

23   *Dudgeon v UK* (1982) 4 EHRR 149.

The approach of the European Court reflects that it is primarily for national authorities to safeguard human rights since they are better placed to evaluate local needs and conditions. There is no universal formula for determining when and how the margin of appreciation should be applied. The width of the discretion will vary according to such factors as the nature of the Convention right (ie, whether it is an absolute, unqualified or a qualified right) and the importance of the particular issue. The margin of appreciation has a limited or no effect where an absolute or unqualified right is concerned, but is likely to be wider when a qualified right is being considered, since these require individual rights to be balanced with the public interest. The Court is more likely to give wide deference to countries in matters concerning their economic or social policy or issues of national security. It has given a narrower discretion to matters concerning criminal procedure, private life or political debate.

10.38   The discretion applied by the UK courts will be, to some extent, different to that of the European Court since they do not have to be so deferential to local conditions. However, the UK courts recognise that they are not always in the best position to dictate how public authorities should best protect human rights. The courts may be guided by a two-stage process.

10.39   Firstly, they will consider the Convention right in question.

(a)   If the right in question concerns an absolute or unqualified right, the courts will be far less likely to give the authorities a discretion than in a situation where a qualified right is in issue.

(b)   If the matter is one where the courts are required to balance individual rights with competing public interests, the courts will be more likely to give a wider discretion to decision makers.

10.40   Secondly, the courts will look at factors which are relevant to the decision making process. The following is a guide to areas that may be of particular interest:

(a)   Do the decisions concern areas that are significantly influenced by resource issues?

(b)   Do the decisions concern social, economic or political spheres where the executive must reconcile competing interests in choosing one policy out of a number that might be acceptable?

(c)   Does the decision concern an area where national authorities have much greater informational resources or a special expertise (the courts will feel more comfortable analysing decisions on criminal justice issues than they will on social issues, such as housing or immigration)?

(d)　　Do the decisions adversely affect those who are most at risk of having their rights compromised, for example, unpopular or vulnerable groups?

The margin of discretion was considered by Lord Hope in a case concerning the deprivation of liberty. He stated that:

> the margin of discretionary judgment that the courts will accord to the executive and Parliament where the right [to liberty] is in issue is narrower than will be appropriate in other contexts. We are not dealing here with matters of social or economic policy, where opinions may reasonably differ in a democratic society and where choices on behalf of the country as a whole are properly left to government and to legislature. We are dealing with actions taken on behalf of society as a whole which affect the rights and freedoms of the individual. This is where the courts may legitimately intervene, to ensure that the actions taken are proportionate. It is an essential safeguard, if individual rights and freedoms are to be protected in a democratic society which respects the principle that minorities, however unpopular, have the same rights as the majority.[24]

10.41　Even where the court gives a degree of deference to decision makers it must always comply with its overriding responsibility to ensure that any decision respects the object and purpose of the Convention.

Decisions based on policies and immunities

Blanket policies

10.42　There are occasions where public authorities have adopted blanket policies with respect to particular situations where they are not prepared to allow discretion or countervailing factors to be considered.

10.43　The incorporation of the Convention into UK law means that it is not possible to blindly follow such policies. Instead, decision makers must make their assessments on a case-by-case basis. Even though a policy will be a significant factor in the process, decision makers will need to ensure that it does not bring about disproportionate results that conflict with the object and purpose of the Convention.

24　*A v Secretary of State for the Home Department* [2005] 2 WLR 87.

> **Case illustration**
>
> A prison service order operated a strict policy that babies could be allowed to remain with their mothers in a Mother and Baby Unit until they were eighteen months old. Thereafter, a strict policy of separation would be operated.
>
> It was decided that the fundamental purpose behind the policy was to promote the interests and welfare of the child. However, the strict policy of separation at eighteen months was found to be unlawful. It was found that if the policy was detrimental to the child's welfare, this would conflict with the very purpose of keeping them with their mothers. The courts also had to balance the effect of the decision on the child's best interests and the right to family life of the child and the adult.[25]

Immunities or privileges

10.44 There are certain situations where public authorities have been granted immunities or privileges from legal actions being brought against them. Where such immunity exists there are two questions that must initially be asked.

(i) Does the immunity or privilege in question pursue a legitimate aim?

(ii) If it does, is the need for the immunity or privilege proportionate to the legitimate aim being pursued.

10.45 This issue has received close consideration where individuals have complained about their inability to bring actions against local authorities for negligence in the exercise of their child welfare functions. The non-existence of a cause of action in this situation was not found to violate the right to a fair trial under article 6(1) of the Convention. The European Court found that the domestic courts did take into consideration the competing interests of public policy issues, (such as the difficulty of the decisions which the authorities sometimes had to make and the expense if every decision could be challenged) with the rights of the individuals affected. The European Court also noted that it only applied to limited aspects of the powers and duties exercised by local authority with respect to child welfare.

---

25 *R v Secretary of State for the Home Department and another ex p P & Q* [2001] 1 WLR 2002.

10.46   However, the European Court found that if the negligence of the authorities resulted in the violation of a right, particularly under articles 2, 3 or 8 of the Convention, an individual must be entitled to bring an action against the local authorities. Therefore, where a local authority failed to separate four children from their mother even though they were aware of the sustained abuse that the children were receiving, the UK was found to have violated article 3 (the prohibition of torture, inhuman and degrading treatment and punishment) in accordance with article 13 (the right to an effective remedy).[26]

10.47   This decision was confirmed in a case where the European Court found that the local authorities had not violated the article 3 or 8 rights of two children, as they could not reasonably have known about the sexual abuse they were suffering. However, the inability of the individuals to even bring an action for the alleged violation of these rights amounted to a violation of the right to an effective remedy under article 13.[27]

10.48   It should be noted that section 7 of the Human Rights Act 1998 provides individuals with a direct right of action for breaches of a Convention right. Section 7(5) states that the action must be brought within a year of being complained of, or any longer period that the court believes is just having regard to all the circumstances.

26 *Z v UK* (2002) 34 EHRR 97.
27 *DC and JS v UK* October 2002 (unreported).

How the Human Rights Act 1998 works

Introduction

11.1   The Human Rights Act 1998 can be divided into two main parts:
(a)   the rights contained in the European Convention which have been adopted into UK law; and
(b)   how the Act is to be applied to UK law.

11.2   The Convention rights do not appear in the main body of the Act but are contained in the first Schedule to the Act. The 22 sections of the Act establish how the Act should be applied. Being a constitutional instrument – that is, an Act which can be applied to all other UK laws – the courts are required to give the Act a generous and far-reaching interpretation in order to ensure that rights are protected to the fullest extent possible.

11.3   It should be noted that two provisions of the European Convention signed by the UK do not appear in the first Schedule to the Human Rights Act. They are articles 1 and 13. Article 1 provides that the rights and freedoms contained in the Convention must be applied to every person in the UK and article 13 provides that domestic courts must provide an effective remedy whenever a Convention right is breached. The Lord Chancellor explained during the Parliamentary debates on the Human Rights Act that there was no need to include these two articles in the first Schedule since they are given effect in the sections of the Human Rights Act 1998.[1]

11.4   This chapter will outline the relationship with and the effect of the Human Rights Act on UK law. It will then consider the definition of 'public authority', paying particular attention to the difficult question of hybrid bodies, for example, those charities and private bodies that may carry out public functions. Finally, the chapter will highlight who can be regarded as a 'victim' under the Act.

The effect of the Human Rights Act on UK law

Interpreting legislation

11.5   There are two particular types of legislation in the UK, primary legislation, which is legislation passed by Acts of Parliament and secondary legislation. Secondary legislation is introduced by

---

1   However, there may be implications from the failure to include those two articles (see para 11.30 below).

government ministers in order to provide the detail which will help ensure the effectiveness of primary legislation. Such secondary legislation will include, among other things, statutory instruments.

> The duty to protect a child's 'special educational needs' is referred to in Part IV of the Education Act 1996. In order to provide an effective legal framework in this area, regulations, such as The Education (Special Educational Needs) (England) (Consolidation) Regulations 2001 have been put in place, and in January 2002, a Special Educational Needs Code of Practice was put in place by the Department of Education and Skills. This guidance has the force of law as it was issued under section 7(1) of the Local Authority Social Services Act 1970.

11.6 Section 3(1) of the Human Rights Act states that all UK legislation must be interpreted in a manner that is compatible with the European Convention, so far as it is possible to do so. Courts and tribunals, therefore, must interpret the legislation so that it is in accordance with the Convention. However, they are not entitled to contort the words or meaning of an Act to the point where it produces an implausible or incredible meaning that is quite different from what Parliament intended. One of the judges in the House of Lords who sought to clarify the position explained that, 'The meaning imported by application of section 3 must be compatible with the underlying thrust of the legislation being construed.'[2]

> **Case illustrations**
>
> The purpose of section 29 of the Crime (Sentences) Act 1997 was to ensure that the Home Secretary could control the release of prisoners serving mandatory life sentences. Although the Home Secretary's involvement was recognised as being in contravention of Article 6 of the European Convention (because the Home Secretary cannot be regarded as an

---

2   Lord Nicholls in *Ghaidan v Mendoza* [2004] 2 AC 557.

independent tribunal) the House of Lords concluded that the purpose of section 29 was so clear that it could not interpret the legislation in any way that would preclude the Home Secretary from setting the minimum period to be served by mandatory life sentence prisoners.[3] Therefore, the Court made a declaration that section 29 was incompatible with article 6 of the European Convention in accordance with section 4 of the Human Rights Act (see para 11.8 below). As a result the Government repealed section 29 and so removed the Home Secretary from the role of setting the minimum term of imprisonment.

G lived in a homosexual relationship with another man who held a flat as a statutory tenant. When his partner died, the landlord claimed that G was not entitled to succeed to the tenancy because the Rent Act 1977 limited the succession to surviving partners in a hetrosexual relationship. He relied on this because the wording of the legislation stated that the successor would be 'as his or her husband or wife' (it had already been established that this included cohabiting hetrosexual relationships). The Court recognised that the distinction on the grounds of sexual orientation had no legitimate aim and was without good reason. In accordance with its powers under section 3 of the Human Rights Act it interpreted the phrase to mean, 'as if they were his wife or husband' so that the legislation could include homosexual relationships.

11.7   Where it is not possible to interpret legislation, the approach of the courts or tribunals will depend on whether it concerns primary or secondary legislation.

Primary legislation

11.8   Courts and tribunals are not entitled to strike down primary legislation. This would be regarded as an over-interference of parliamentary sovereignty by the judiciary. Instead the courts will be able to make a 'declaration of incompatibility' in accordance with

3   *R on the application of Anderson v Secretary of State for the Home Department* [2003] 1 AC 837.

section 4 of the Human Rights Act. Making a declaration has the effect of informing Parliament that a piece of legislation contravenes the Convention. It does not force Parliament to do anything to remedy the breach.[4] However, Parliament runs the risk of having complaints brought directly to the European Court, if it does not replace the 'offending' piece of legislation so that it is compatible. The declaration by the House of Lords that section 23 of the Anti-Terrorism Crime and Security Act was incompatible with Article 5 and Article 14 of the European Convention on Human Rights resulted in the government releasing the prisoners and instead placing them under 'control orders'.[5]

11.9   There are slight variations in the application of the Human Rights Act in Scotland, Wales and Northern Ireland. Declarations of incompatibility apply to Acts made by the English Parliament, which are enforceable in Scotland, Northern Ireland and Wales. However, declarations do not apply to Acts passed by the Scottish Parliament. Instead, incompatible legislation will be struck down on the grounds that the Scottish Parliament has incorrectly applied its powers. This is also true of Wales and Northern Ireland, where the respective Assemblies cannot take executive action that is incompatible with the Convention. However, section 21(1) of the Human Rights Act states that in Northern Ireland, any constitutional law instrument, as opposed to a regular parliamentary Act made by the Northern Ireland Assembly will be treated in the same way as primary legislation under English law.

Secondary legislation

11.10   Where it is not possible to interpret secondary legislation in a manner which is compatible with the Convention, the courts have the power to override or disregard that piece of legislation. There is no need to make a declaration of incompatibility. However, in very rare circumstances, secondary legislation may need to be worded in such a way in order to give effect to the primary legislation. In such a situation the courts will need to make a declaration of incompatibility if there is no other way in which the legislation can be interpreted compatibly with the Convention.

4   Parliament does not have to comply with the Convention because it is not regarded as a public authority under section 6(3)(b) of the Human Rights Act 1998.

5   See *A v Secretary of State for the Home Department* [2005] 2 WLR 87 and Chapter 9, note 31, above.

Common law

11.11   Common law is not made by Parliament. It develops through interpretation by judges. It is underpinned by a system of judicial precedent, which means that the judiciary is usually obliged to follow the principles established in previous decisions. The decision of a higher court is binding on the lower courts.

> Parliament has so far declined to adopt legislation on areas concerning privacy. The law in this area has developed through common law cases on defamation and breach of confidence and not through legislation adopted by Parliament.

11.12   Section 6(1) of the Human Rights Act states that it is unlawful for a public authority to act in a way which is incompatible with a Convention right. The courts are under a duty to comply with the Convention because they are defined as a public authority in section 6(3)(a). This means that they are under a duty to disregard any existing common law decisions that infringe with the Convention in order to ensure its compatibility. Judicial precedent cannot be relied upon to exclude a Convention right.

The importance of the case law of the European Convention on Human Rights

11.13   The Human Rights Act 1998 does not mean that the UK courts will have to begin the process of establishing human rights principles from scratch. When considering a human rights issue, the courts will be able to consider the vast amount of case law that has developed from the Strasbourg tribunal.[6]

11.14   Section 2 of the 1998 Act states that the domestic courts should take Strasbourg jurisprudence into account when making any decision. This does not just mean those cases relating to the UK, but to any country within the Council of Europe. This is because, whatever the differing approach to the law by different European countries, the European Court seeks to establish human rights

---

6   This includes decisions by the European Commission on Human Rights which has been abolished in an effort to streamline the Strasbourg procedure.

principles of general application rather than just a narrow consideration of the case before them.

11.15   The fact that the courts are obliged to take Strasbourg cases 'into account' rather than to 'follow' them means that the courts are not bound by those decisions. This does not, however, provide the UK courts with the opportunity to consider, but then reject, human rights standards set by the European Court. It was made clear when the Human Rights Bill was being debated in Parliament that this section was not designed to permit the UK courts to develop standards that fall below the existing human rights standards established by Strasbourg. It only entitles the UK courts to adopt greater human rights standards than those set out in Strasbourg. Section 2 is phrased in that way because those drafting the Act recognised that human rights are not static but are evolving as society develops.[7] In particular, social values that might have been held previously may change over time.[8]

To whom does the Human Right Act apply?

11.16   The general rule is that individuals and private bodies are entitled to rely on the rights and freedoms contained in the Convention. Conversely, public authorities do not have rights and freedoms under the Convention. Instead, they are under a duty to ensure that they act or refrain from acting in a manner that protects individuals or private bodies from a violation of their rights.

11.17   Individual or private bodies cannot directly bring an action under the Human Rights Act against each other. However, since courts and tribunals have a duty under section 6(3)(a) of the Act to ensure that Convention rights are protected, a violation may be found against the authorities for not protecting the rights of one person from abuse by another.[9]

11.18   The following sections will examine which bodies are regarded as public authorities under the Act, and who has victim status.

---

7   See para 10.10.
8   See *Goodwin v UK* (2002) 35 EHRR 447 referred to at para 10.10.
9   See positive obligations paras 9.19 – 9.29.

What is a 'public authority' under the Human Rights Act?

11.19   Section 6(1) of the Human Rights Act makes it unlawful for a public authority to act in a manner which is incompatible with Convention rights unless it is required to do so by primary legislation that cannot be interpreted any other way.[10]

11.20   Possibly the most contentious aspect of all the sections in the Human Rights Act surrounds the definition of 'public authority'. The greatest debate has concerned the meaning of what are often called hybrid bodies, charities or private bodies carrying out functions of a public nature. To highlight the distinction, pure public authorities will be referred to as 'public sector organisations', while charities or private bodies carrying out public function, will be referred to as 'hybrid bodies'.

Public sector organisations

11.21   The Human Rights Act does not provide a definition of what would be a public sector organisation. During the drafting of the Bill, it was argued that it would be easy to recognise a public sector organisation. All acts of public sector organisations will be subject to the Human Rights Act.[11] The common feature of all public sector organisations is that they share the characteristic that they are accountable to the UK public. Drawing from the case law in Strasbourg, a judge in the House of Lords stated that the test as to whether a person or body is a 'pure' public authority depends on whether it was established with a view to public administration as part of the process of government. The judge concluded as a result that the Parochial Church Council was not a pure public authority under this test.[12]

---

10   See paras 11.6 – 11.8.

11   Although, employees cannot claim civil fair trial rights against public sector employers. See para 8.62.

12   Lord Hope judgment in *Aston Cantlow and Wilmcote with Billesley Parochial Church Council v Wallbank* [2004] 1 AC 546.

Examples of public sector organisations include:

- Central government
- Local government
- The police
- Prisons
- Health authorities
- NHS Trusts
- Immigration service
- Courts and tribunals
- Data Protection Registrar
- Security services and Interception of Communication Commissioners
- Planning inspectorate
- English Heritage
- Statutory regulatory bodies
- Executive agencies
- Parliamentary Commissioner
- Local Government Ombudsman
- Legal Services Commission

Hybrid Bodies

11.22   The government recognised that the Human Rights Act must be wide enough to take account of the increasingly large number of private bodies, such as companies and charities that now carry out public functions that were previously exercised by public sector organisations. This is in accordance with the view of the European Court. It has stated that countries cannot relinquish their responsibilities by delegating them to private bodies.[13] Hybrid bodies are responsible under the Human Rights Act for their public functions, but not for functions which they carry out in their private capacity.

11.23   The most difficult issue to determine is whether charities or private bodies are carrying out functions of a public nature.

---

13   *Costello-Roberts v UK* (1993) 19 EHRR 112.

Examples of hybrid bodies given by the Government during the debates on the Human Rights Bill include:

- Press Complaints Commission
- BBC
- Privatised utilities (eg, British Gas)
- General practitioners

11.24 There have been two particular cases which have considered different situations raising the issue of whether private bodies carrying out public functions are hybrid bodies. The first situation is where a private body takes over a function previously carried out by a public authority. The second is where a public authority delegates some of its duties to a private body.

Case illustration

In *Poplar Housing and Regeneration Community Association Ltd v Donoghue*,[14] the tenant was a non-secure tenant of a housing authority when her property, together with most of the local authority's housing stock was transferred to the Association. The court decided that although the Association was a private body, the Human Rights Act was applicable as it was carrying out a public function. The court looked at the functions they carried out, their funding and their relationship with the local housing authority.

However, the court stated that although the local authority had transferred its housing stock to the Association, its primary public duties had not been transferred. The Association was merely the means by which the local authority sought to perform its public duties.

11.25 However, the fact that a body is subject to a statutory regulation in the performance of its functions does not necessarily mean that they have a public function.

---

14 [2001] 3 WLR 183.

Case illustration

Some residents of the Leonard Cheshire Foundation, a charity which runs residential nursing homes for people with disabilities, claimed that the decision to close the home in their area violated article 8. They had been placed in the home by local authority social services in accordance with their duties. The court held that the Leonard Cheshire Foundation in providing accommodation to those to whom the authority owed a statutory duty was not performing a public function. They stated that the Convention did not intend to make a charity or private body directly liable for the breach. It was not performing a public function, since there was no real difference in the nature of the services provided to privately funded or local authority funded residents. The degree of public funding they received was relevant but not determinative.[15] This means that the responsibility for a Convention breach is with the local authority and not the charity or private body.

The court stated that in future, it would be open for local authorities and the charity or private body providing the service to enter into a contract to fully protect the Convention rights of the residents.

The following factors have been regarded as relevant by the courts in determining whether a charity or private body is carrying out a public function.

- Are they acting under statutory authority?
- Has statutory responsibility been imposed on the core functions of the charity or private body?
- To what extent has the public authority delegated its powers to the charity or private body?

15 *R on the application of Heather and others v Leonard Cheshire Foundation* [2002] HRLR 832.

> - How close is the relationship between the public authority and the charity or private body? In particular, what is the extent of the control or influence which the public authority may be able to exercise over the other body?
> - In addition, the provision of public funding for the activity being carried out by the charity or private body may be relevant.

11.26   The courts have not taken the approach of simply looking at the 'functions' which are being carried out in order to determine whether the charity or private body can be defined as hybrid. The decisions of the courts have differed from the intentions set out by the government when the Human Rights Bill was being debated. The government seemed to suggest that a functional approach was to be taken. This would be in accordance with the duty on states to give Convention rights a wide and generous interpretation. The approach of the courts does not take into account that service users have no choice in the decision of local authorities to contract out their obligations. It also means that they may lose out on an effective remedy in circumstances where their rights are violated. Saying that public authorities which contract out will remain the subject of state responsibility did not assist the residents in the Leonard Cheshire Foundation case, as the local authority was unable to remedy the problem, ie, the closing of the home. Nor is it clear how contractual obligations would assist with unforeseen contingencies.

11.27   A developing body of opinion argues that the courts should adopt a functional approach. In a comprehensive paper on the subject presented at the JUSTICE lectures,[16] Kate Markus, barrister, suggested that the courts should first look at the nature of the function being carried out. She argued that a charity or private body should be regarded as hybrid where the government has provided for the performance of the function by law or whether the function is designed to meet the public interest. This would catch many more organisations than the approach taken by the courts. It would include private residential care homes and possibly extend to those

16   K Markus, 'What is Public Power? The Courts' Approach to the Public Authority Definition under the Human Rights Act'. The lecture was given on 28 May 2002.

providing bed and breakfast accommodation for homeless people. Markus states:

> It is hard to justify their not being liable. They deliver important services to the public, forming part of a framework of provision which the state has determined should exist; in the course of doing so they have the potential to violate fundamental rights; they undertake the activities freely and for their own profit or self-interest; they are capable of assessing whether they can deliver services in a Convention compliant manner. If entrepreneurs choose to enter the field of public provision why should they not be liable if they violate Convention rights in doing so?

11.28 This matter was considered by the House of Lords in a case concerning an 84-year-old woman, Y, living in a nursing home. The home was part of an organisation that provided approximately 29,000 care home beds in the UK, 80 per cent of which were fully or partly funded by local authorities. The care home decided to terminate the placement in the light of allegations concerning Y's husband towards the staff. The preliminary issue was whether the care home should be treated as a public or a private body. The House of Lords decided by 3 votes to 2 that the privately owned care home was not carrying out public functions. The reasons given by the judges highlighted the contentious nature of the subject and differed even amongst the majority. However, their key consideration was that the private home was simply providing a service for which it charged a commercial fee. It was also stated that even where a state has delegated responsibility for providing a service to a private body there may be state and other functions to which it remains responsible as part of a three-way contract between the State, the private body and the individual. The judges who were in the minority highlighted that the relevant legislation on residential care made clear that the intention of Parliament is to make provision for very vulnerable sections of the community.[17]

11.29 It is very unlikely that this decision will settle the on-going debate that surrounds this issue. The interpretation given to the meaning of a public body by the Courts still appears to be far narrower than the intended meaning when the Bill was being discussed by Parliament. There is a clear gap in human rights protection to those who, for example, receive residential care from a state run as opposed to a

---

17 See *Johnson and others v Havering London Borough Council and others* [2007] 3 WLR 112.

private care home. Lord Neuberger summed up the policy considerations that lay behind the decision when he stated:

> It is thought to be desirable, in some circumstances, to encourage core public authorities to contract-out services, and it may well be inimical to that policy if section 6(1) automatically applied to the contractor as it would to the authority. Indeed, unattractive thought it may be to some people, one of the purposes of contracting-out at least certain services previously performed by local authorities may be to avoid some of the legal constraints and disadvantages which apply to local authorities but not to private contractors.[18]

11.30   The decision by the UK courts is also more restrictive than the decisions set out in case law from the European Court, mainly because Articles 1 and 13 of the European Convention (which concern the obligation to secure Convention rights for everyone within the State's jurisdiction and to provide the right to an effective remedy) are not included in the Human Rights Act.[19]

11.31   The decision of the majority of the Court appears to both assume that individuals placed in a private care home will be able to assert their Convention rights against public bodies and that any contractual agreement will guarantee the individual's Convention rights. But the Joint Committee on Human Rights, which has written two very comprehensive reports on the meaning of the term 'public authority' under the Human Rights Act, has expressed considerable concern that individuals will not be able to rely on the full protection of their human rights through contractual terms.

11.32   Nor has litigation managed to end the debate. Indeed, prior to the decision by the House of Lords, the second report of the Joint Committee took the view that the Court's decision would be 'unlikely to lead to an enduring and effective solution to the interpretative problems associated with the meaning of public authority.'[20] Although the previous Joint Committee report had not been in favour of amending the Human Rights Act so as to make clear the definition of public authority, the second report indicated that the

---

18   Para 152.

19   For instance, the European Court of Human Rights held that the infliction of corporal punishment in a private school was a matter engaging State responsibility under the Convention (*Costello-Roberts v UK* (1993) 19 EHRR 112).

20   Joint Committee on Human Rights, *The Meaning of Public Authority under the Human Rights Act* (Ninth Report of Session 2006–07, 19 March 2007), p41.

time had now come to bring forward a legislative solution. Its conclusion states:

> We consider that the current situation is unsatisfactory and unfair and continues to frustrate the intention of Parliament. It creates the potential for significant inconsistencies in the application of the HRA and denies the protection of the rights it guarantees to those who most need its protection. In view of the continuing trend towards the contracting out of public functions, there is now a need for urgent action to secure a solution and to reinstate the application of the HRA in accordance with Parliament's intention under the Human Rights Act.[21]

11.33 There are indications that the Government may be moving towards this view. The then Department for Constitutional Affairs joined itself as a party in the case before the House of Lords in order to argue that the care home was exercising functions of a public nature. However, this view was not accepted by the majority of the Court. One of the judges commented that:

> It may well be thought to be desirable that residents in privately owned care homes should be given Convention rights against the proprietors. That is a subject on which there are no doubt opposing views, and I am in no position to express an opinion. However, if the legislature considers such a course appropriate, then it would be right to spell it out in terms, and, in the process, to make it clear whether should be enjoyed by all residents of such care homes, or only certain classes (eg those whose care and accommodation is wholly or partly funded by a local authority).[22]

11.34 In light of its lack of success in the Courts, the Government may seek to resolve this issue by amending the legislation in order to define the meaning of a public authority.

The effect of the Convention on private individuals and bodies

11.35 Private individuals have no responsibility to protect Convention rights under the Human Rights Act. However, there is a positive obligation on public authorities to ensure that these rights are protected through its criminal and civil law.

---

21 Ibid at pp52–53.
22 Lord Neuberger ibid at para 171.

> **Case illustration**
>
> The European Court held that the UK was in violation of the Convention for not providing adequate criminal law provisions to protect a child who was beaten by his stepfather with a garden cane.[23]

Who has victim status under the Human Rights Act 1998?

11.36   Any person, corporate body, non-governmental organisation, or group of individuals may claim that their rights have been contravened under the Act. It is not necessary to be a UK national in order to make a claim under the Convention. For example, asylum-seekers will be entitled to rely on Convention rights. The general rule is that a person has to be within the country in order to claim their Convention rights against the state. The Convention will also apply in a situation where the removal of a person from the UK will place them at risk of serious or irreparable harm abroad.

> **Case illustration**
>
> A person who was not given leave to remain in the UK could not be deported back to the country from which he had fled, because there was a clear risk that he would be subjected to interrogation that would amount to torture or inhuman treatment if returned. This would amount to a violation of article 3 of the Convention.[24]

When does a person have victim status?

11.37   The rules for establishing when a person may claim their rights are not specifically set out under the Human Rights Act. Instead, section 7 of the Act defers to the approach established by the Strasbourg

23 *A v UK* (1998) 27 EHRR 611.
24 *Chahal v UK* (1996) 23 EHRR 413.

tribunal. Although, the European Convention does not define who is regarded as a victim, there are certain principles that have emerged from the decisions of the Strasbourg tribunal.

11.38 The general rule is that a person will have to be directly affected by an act or an omission in order to be regarded as a victim. This does not always mean that a person will need to be affected by a detrimental act before they can make a claim.

Case illustration

Two women were entitled to challenge legislation restricting abortion even though they were not pregnant. They stated that the effect of the legislation meant that they must either, renounce sexual intercourse, use contraceptive measures or run the risk of unwanted offspring. They had victim status because the legislation affected their article 8(1) right to private life. Article 8(1) comprises the right to establish and develop relationships with other humans for the development and fulfilment of their own personality. This has been found to include sexual life. It was enough that their rights were at risk of being affected, and they did not need to show that they had suffered detriment as a result of the legislation.[25]

11.39 The more serious and irreparable the risk of harm, the greater is the likelihood that a person will be considered a victim for the purpose of the Convention. Serious and irreparable harm are usually concerned with well-being (articles 2 and 3).[26]

11.40 There are some situations where it is impossible for a person to know whether or not their rights are being infringed. This is often the case where a person is being subjected to secret surveillance. If the approach of the authorities is so broad that, for instance, all users of postal or telecommunications services are directly affected, they may all qualify as victims.[27]

11.41 In spite of the general rule, there are circumstances where a person may make a claim under the Convention even though they are only indirectly affected.

---

25 *Bruggemann and Scheuten v Germany* (1976) 5 DR 103.
26 *Soering v UK* (1989) 11 EHRR 439.
27 *Klass v Germany* (1980) 2 EHRR 214.

> **Case illustration**
>
> A man who wanted to contest his wife's decision to have an abortion was considered to have victim status, even though his claim did not succeed. However, where a man who wanted to contest the abortion laws even though he was not an expectant father was not considered to be a victim. The difference in this case was that there was a real rather than a hypothetical pregnancy to be considered, and it was necessary to consider the paternity rights of the father.[28]

11.42   A person may be an indirect victim in a situation where they have suffered as a result of the violation of the Convention rights of another person. For example, relations have been allowed to bring claims following the death of a husband, unmarried sibling and child.

From what date does the Human Rights Act 1998 apply?

11.43   Although the Act received Royal Assent on 9 November 1998, it only came into force on 2 October 2000. In general, the act or omission that is alleged to have contravened a Convention right must have occurred on or after the 2 October 2000 in order to have them determined by the UK courts. This is set out in section 22 of the Act.

11.44   However, where the act or omission started prior to the 2 October 2000 but is still continuing after that date, the Human Rights Act will apply. Therefore, a person in residential care who has been kept in conditions which violate their article 3 or article 8 rights will be able to rely on the Convention even if they had first been subjected to those conditions prior to the date when the Act entered into force.

11.45   On the other hand, if an individual, or a charity or private body (not acting in the course of its public functions) is taken to court by a public authority, they are entitled to argue in their defence that a Convention right has been contravened whenever it occurred. It does not matter that the act or omission took place prior to the entry into force of the Human Rights Act.

28   *Paton v UK* (1980) 19 DR 24.

PART III

Human Rights Act 1998

Human Rights Act 1998

INTRODUCTION

The Convention Rights

1(1) In this Act 'the Convention rights' means the rights and fundamental freedoms set out in –

(a) Articles 2 to 12 and 14 of the Convention,

(b) Articles 1 to 3 of the First Protocol, and

(c) Articles 1 and 2 of the Sixth Protocol,

as read with Articles 16 to 18 of the Convention.

(2) Those Articles are to have effect for the purposes of this Act subject to any designated derogation or reservation (as to which see sections 14 and 15).

(3) The Articles are set out in Schedule 1.

(4) The Secretary of State may by order make such amendments to this Act as he considers appropriate to reflect the effect, in relation to the United Kingdom, of a protocol.

(5) In subsection (4) 'protocol' means a protocol to the Convention –

(a) which the United Kingdom has ratified; or

(b) which the United Kingdom has signed with a view to ratification.

(6) No amendment may be made by an order under subsection (4) so as to come into force before the protocol concerned is in force in relation to the United Kingdom.

Interpretation of Convention rights

2(1) A court or tribunal determining a question which has arisen in connection with a Convention right must take into account any –

(a) judgment, decision, declaration or advisory opinion of the European Court of Human Rights,

(b) opinion of the Commission given in a report adopted under Article 31 of the Convention,

(c) decision of the Commission in connection with Article 26 or 27(2) of the Convention, or

(d) decision of the Committee of Ministers taken under Article 46 of the Convention,

whenever made or given, so far as, in the opinion of the court or tribunal, it is relevant to the proceedings in which that question has arisen.

(2)   Evidence of any judgment, decision, declaration or opinion of which account may have to be taken under this section is to be given in proceedings before any court or tribunal in such manner as may be provided by rules.

(3)   In this section 'rules' means rules of court or, in the case of proceedings before a tribunal, rules made for the purposes of this section –

(a)   by the Lord Chancellor or the Secretary of State, in relation to any proceedings outside Scotland;

(b)   by the Secretary of State, in relation to proceedings in Scotland; or

(c)   by a Northern Ireland department, in relation to proceedings before a tribunal in Northern Ireland –

(i)   which deals with transferred matters; and

(ii)   for which no rules made under paragraph (a) are in force.

LEGISLATION

Interpretation of legislation

3(1)   So far as it is possible to do so, primary legislation and subordinate legislation must be read and given effect in a way which is compatible with the Convention rights.

(2)   This section –

(a)   applies to primary legislation and subordinate legislation whenever enacted;

(b)   does not affect the validity, continuing operation or enforcement of any incompatible primary legislation; and

(c)   does not affect the validity, continuing operation or enforcement of any incompatible subordinate legislation if (disregarding any possibility of revocation) primary legislation prevents removal of the incompatibility.

Declaration of incompatibility

4(1)   Subsection (2) applies in any proceedings in which a court determines whether a provision of primary legislation is compatible with a Convention right.

(2)   If the court is satisfied that the provision is incompatible with a Convention right, it may make a declaration of that incompatibility.

(3)   Subsection (4) applies in any proceedings in which a court determines whether a provision of subordinate legislation, made in the exercise of a power conferred by primary legislation, is compatible with a Convention right.

(4)   If the court is satisfied –

(a)   that the provision is incompatible with a Convention right, and

(b)   that (disregarding any possibility of revocation) the primary legislation concerned prevents removal of the incompatibility,

it may make a declaration of that incompatibility.

(5)   In this section 'court' means –

(a)   the House of Lords;

(b)   the Judicial Committee of the Privy Council;

(c)   the Courts-Martial Appeal Court;

(d) in Scotland, the High Court of Justiciary sitting otherwise than as a trial court or the Court of Session;

e) in England and Wales or Northern Ireland, the High Court or the Court of Appeal.

(6) A declaration under this section ('a declaration of incompatibility') –

(a) does not affect the validity, continuing operation or enforcement of the provision in respect of which it is given; and

(b) is not binding on the parties to the proceedings in which it is made.

Right of Crown to intervene

5(1) Where a court is considering whether to make a declaration of incompatibility, the Crown is entitled to notice in accordance with rules of court.

(2) In any case to which subsection (1) applies –

(a) a Minister of the Crown (or a person nominated by him),

(b) a member of the Scottish Executive,

(c) a Northern Ireland Minister,

(d) a Northern Ireland department,

is entitled, on giving notice in accordance with rules of court, to be joined as a party to the proceedings.

(3) Notice under subsection (2) may be given at any time during the proceedings.

(4) A person who has been made a party to criminal proceedings (other than in Scotland) as the result of a notice under subsection (2) may, with leave, appeal to the House of Lords against any declaration of incompatibility made in the proceedings.

(5) In subsection (4) –

'criminal proceedings' includes all proceedings before the Courts-Martial Appeal Court; and

'leave' means leave granted by the court making the declaration of incompatibility or by the House of Lords.

PUBLIC AUTHORITIES

Acts of public authorities

6(1) It is unlawful for a public authority to act in a way which is incompatible with a Convention right.

(2) Subsection (1) does not apply to an act if –

(a) as the result of one or more provisions of primary legislation, the authority could not have acted differently; or

(b) in the case of one or more provisions of, or made under, primary legislation which cannot be read or given effect in a way which is compatible with the Convention rights, the authority was acting so as to give effect to or enforce those provisions.

(3) In this section 'public authority' includes –

(a) a court or tribunal, and

(b) any person certain of whose functions are functions of a public nature, but does not include either House of Parliament or a person exercising functions in connection with proceedings in Parliament.

(4) In subsection (3) 'Parliament' does not include the House of Lords in its judicial capacity.

(5) In relation to a particular act, a person is not a public authority by virtue only of subsection (3)(b) if the nature of the act is private.

(6) 'An act' includes a failure to act but does not include a failure to –

(a) introduce in, or lay before, Parliament a proposal for legislation; or

(b) make any primary legislation or remedial order.

Proceedings

7(1) A person who claims that a public authority has acted (or proposes to act) in a way which is made unlawful by section 6(1) may –

(a) bring proceedings against the authority under this Act in the appropriate court or tribunal, or

(b) rely on the Convention right or rights concerned in any legal proceedings,

but only if he is (or would be) a victim of the unlawful act.

(2) In subsection (1)(a) 'appropriate court or tribunal' means such court or tribunal as may be determined in accordance with rules; and proceedings against an authority include a counterclaim or similar proceeding.

(3) If the proceedings are brought on an application for judicial review, the applicant is to be taken to have a sufficient interest in relation to the unlawful act only if he is, or would be, a victim of that act.

(4) If the proceedings are made by way of a petition for judicial review in Scotland, the applicant shall be taken to have title and interest to sue in relation to the unlawful act only if he is, or would be, a victim of that act.

(5) Proceedings under subsection (1)(a) must be brought before the end of –

(a) the period of one year beginning with the date on which the act complained of took place; or

(b) such longer period as the court or tribunal considers equitable having regard to all the circumstances,

but that is subject to any rule imposing a stricter time limit in relation to the procedure in question.

(6) In subsection (1)(b) 'legal proceedings' includes –

(a) proceedings brought by or at the instigation of a public authority; and

(b) an appeal against the decision of a court or tribunal.

(7) For the purposes of this section, a person is a victim of an unlawful act only if he would be a victim for the purposes of Article 34 of the Convention if proceedings were brought in the European Court of Human Rights in respect of that act.

(8) Nothing in this Act creates a criminal offence.

(9) In this section 'rules' means –

(a) in relation to proceedings before a court or tribunal outside Scotland, rules made by the Lord Chancellor or the Secretary of State for the purposes of this section or rules of court,

(b) in relation to proceedings before a court or tribunal in Scotland, rules made by the Secretary of State for those purposes,

(c) in relation to proceedings before a tribunal in Northern Ireland –

(i) which deals with transferred matters; and

(ii) for which no rules made under paragraph (a) are in force,

rules made by a Northern Ireland department for those purposes,

and includes provision made by order under section 1 of the Courts and Legal Services Act 1990.

(10) In making rules, regard must be had to section 9.

(11) The Minister who has power to make rules in relation to a particular tribunal may, to the extent he considers it necessary to ensure that the tribunal can provide an appropriate remedy in relation to an act (or proposed act) of a public authority which is (or would be) unlawful as a result of section 6(1), by order add to –

(a) the relief or remedies which the tribunal may grant; or

(b) the grounds on which it may grant any of them.

(12) An order made under subsection (11) may contain such incidental, supplemental, consequential or transitional provision as the Minister making it considers appropriate.

(13) 'The Minister' includes the Northern Ireland department concerned.

Judicial remedies

8(1) In relation to any act (or proposed act) of a public authority which the court finds is (or would be) unlawful, it may grant such relief or remedy, or make such order, within its powers as it considers just and appropriate.

(2) But damages may be awarded only by a court which has power to award damages, or to order the payment of compensation, in civil proceedings.

(3) No award of damages is to be made unless, taking account of all the circumstances of the case, including –

(a) any other relief or remedy granted, or order made, in relation to the act in question (by that or any other court), and

(b) the consequences of any decision (of that or any other court) in respect of that act,

the court is satisfied that the award is necessary to afford just satisfaction to the person in whose favour it is made.

(4) In determining –

(a) whether to award damages, or

(b) the amount of an award,

the court must take into account the principles applied by the European Court of Human Rights in relation to the award of compensation under Article 41 of the Convention.

(5) A public authority against which damages are awarded is to be treated –

(a) in Scotland, for the purposes of section 3 of the Law Reform (Miscellaneous Provisions) (Scotland) Act 1940 as if the award were made in an action of damages in which the authority has been found liable in respect of loss or damage to the person to whom the award is made;

(b) for the purposes of the Civil Liability (Contribution) Act 1978 as liable in respect of damage suffered by the person to whom the award is made.

(6) In this section –

'court' includes a tribunal;

'damages' means damages for an unlawful act of a public authority; and

'unlawful' means unlawful under section 6(1).

Judicial acts

9(1) Proceedings under section 7(1)(a) in respect of a judicial act may be brought only –

(a) by exercising a right of appeal;

(b) on an application (in Scotland a petition) for judicial review; or

(c) in such other forum as may be prescribed by rules.

(2) That does not affect any rule of law which prevents a court from being the subject of judicial review.

(3) In proceedings under this Act in respect of a judicial act done in good faith, damages may not be awarded otherwise than to compensate a person to the extent required by Article 5(5) of the Convention.

(4) An award of damages permitted by subsection (3) is to be made against the Crown; but no award may be made unless the appropriate person, if not a party to the proceedings, is joined.

(5) In this section –

'appropriate person' means the Minister responsible for the court concerned, or a person or government department nominated by him;

'court' includes a tribunal;

'judge' includes a member of a tribunal, a justice of the peace and a clerk or other officer entitled to exercise the jurisdiction of a court;

'judicial act' means a judicial act of a court and includes an act done on the instructions, or on behalf, of a judge; and

'rules' has the same meaning as in section 7(9).

REMEDIAL ACTION

Power to take remedial action

10(1) This section applies if –

(a) a provision of legislation has been declared under section 4 to be incompatible with a Convention right and, if an appeal lies –

(i) all persons who may appeal have stated in writing that they do not intend to do so;

(ii) the time for bringing an appeal has expired and no appeal has been brought within that time; or

(iii) an appeal brought within that time has been determined or abandoned; or

(b) it appears to a Minister of the Crown or Her Majesty in Council that, having regard to a finding of the European Court of Human Rights made after the coming into force of this section in proceedings against the United Kingdom, a provision of legislation is incompatible with an obligation of the United Kingdom arising from the Convention.

(2) If a Minister of the Crown considers that there are compelling reasons for proceeding under this section, he may by order make such amendments to the legislation as he considers necessary to remove the incompatibility.

(3) If, in the case of subordinate legislation, a Minister of the Crown considers –

(a) that it is necessary to amend the primary legislation under which the subordinate legislation in question was made, in order to enable the incompatibility to be removed, and

(b) that there are compelling reasons for proceeding under this section,

he may by order make such amendments to the primary legislation as he considers necessary.

(4) This section also applies where the provision in question is in subordinate legislation and has been quashed, or declared invalid, by reason of incompatibility with a Convention right and the Minister proposes to proceed under paragraph 2(b) of Schedule 2.

(5) If the legislation is an Order in Council, the power conferred by subsection (2) or (3) is exercisable by Her Majesty in Council.

(6) In this section 'legislation' does not include a Measure of the Church Assembly or of the General Synod of the Church of England.

(7) Schedule 2 makes further provision about remedial orders.

OTHER RIGHTS AND PROCEEDINGS

Safeguard for existing human rights

11 A person's reliance on a Convention right does not restrict –

(a) any other right or freedom conferred on him by or under any law having effect in any part of the United Kingdom; or

(b) his right to make any claim or bring any proceedings which he could make or bring apart from sections 7 to 9.

Freedom of expression

12(1) This section applies if a court is considering whether to grant any relief which, if granted, might affect the exercise of the Convention right to freedom of expression.

(2) If the person against whom the application for relief is made ('the respondent') is neither present nor represented, no such relief is to be granted unless the court is satisfied –

(a) that the applicant has taken all practicable steps to notify the respondent; or

(b) that there are compelling reasons why the respondent should not be notified.

(3) No such relief is to be granted so as to restrain publication before trial unless the court is satisfied that the applicant is likely to establish that publication should not be allowed.

(4) The court must have particular regard to the importance of the Convention right to freedom of expression and, where the proceedings relate to material

which the respondent claims, or which appears to the court, to be journalistic, literary or artistic material (or to conduct connected with such material), to –

(a) the extent to which –
  (i) the material has, or is about to, become available to the public; or
  (ii) it is, or would be, in the public interest for the material to be published;
(b) any relevant privacy code.

(5) In this section –
'court' includes a tribunal; and
'relief' includes any remedy or order (other than in criminal proceedings).

Freedom of thought, conscience and religion

13(1) If a court's determination of any question arising under this Act might affect the exercise by a religious organisation (itself or its members collectively) of the Convention right to freedom of thought, conscience and religion, it must have particular regard to the importance of that right.

(2) In this section 'court' includes a tribunal.

DEROGATIONS AND RESERVATIONS

Derogations

14(1) In this Act 'designated derogation' means any derogation by the United Kingdom from an Article of the Convention, or of any protocol to the Convention, which is designated for the purposes of this Act in an order made by the Secretary of State.

[(2) *repealed.*]

(3) If a designated derogation is amended or replaced it ceases to be a designated derogation.

(4) But subsection (3) does not prevent the Secretary of State from exercising his power under subsection (1) to make a fresh designation order in respect of the Article concerned.

(5) The Secretary of State must by order make such amendments to Schedule 3 as he considers appropriate to reflect –
(a) any designation order; or
(b) the effect of subsection (3).

(6) A designation order may be made in anticipation of the making by the United Kingdom of a proposed derogation.

Reservations

15(1) In this Act 'designated reservation' means –
(a) the United Kingdom's reservation to Article 2 of the First Protocol to the Convention; and
(b) any other reservation by the United Kingdom to an Article of the Convention, or of any protocol to the Convention, which is designated for the purposes of this Act in an order made by the Secretary of State.

(2) The text of the reservation referred to in subsection (1)(a) is set out in Part II of Schedule 3.

(3) If a designated reservation is withdrawn wholly or in part it ceases to be a designated reservation.

(4) But subsection (3) does not prevent the Secretary of State from exercising his power under subsection (1)(b) to make a fresh designation order in respect of the Article concerned.

(5) The Secretary of State must by order make such amendments to this Act as he considers appropriate to reflect –

(a) any designation order; or

(b) the effect of subsection (3).

Period for which designated derogations have effect

16(1) If it has not already been withdrawn by the United Kingdom, a designated derogation ceases to have effect for the purposes of this Act in the case of any other derogation, at the end of the period of five years beginning with the date on which the order designating it was made.

(2) At any time before the period –

(a) fixed by subsection (1), or

(b) extended by an order under this subsection,

comes to an end, the Secretary of State may by order extend it by a further period of five years.

(3) An order under section 14(1) ceases to have effect at the end of the period for consideration, unless a resolution has been passed by each House approving the order.

(4) Subsection (3) does not affect –

(a) anything done in reliance on the order; or

(b) the power to make a fresh order under section 14(1).

(5) In subsection (3) 'period for consideration' means the period of forty days beginning with the day on which the order was made.

(6) In calculating the period for consideration, no account is to be taken of any time during which –

(a) Parliament is dissolved or prorogued; or

(b) both Houses are adjourned for more than four days.

(7) If a designated derogation is withdrawn by the United Kingdom, the Secretary of State must by order make such amendments to this Act as he considers are required to reflect that withdrawal.

Periodic review of designated reservations

17(1) The appropriate Minister must review the designated reservation referred to in section 15(1)(a) –

(a) before the end of the period of five years beginning with the date on which section 1(2) came into force; and

(b) if that designation is still in force, before the end of the period of five years beginning with the date on which the last report relating to it was laid under subsection (3).

(2)   The appropriate Minister must review each of the other designated reservations (if any) –

(a) before the end of the period of five years beginning with the date on which the order designating the reservation first came into force; and

(b) if the designation is still in force, before the end of the period of five years beginning with the date on which the last report relating to it was laid under subsection (3).

(3)   The Minister conducting a review under this section must prepare a report on the result of the review and lay a copy of it before each House of Parliament.

Appointment to European Court of Human Rights

18(1) In this section 'judicial office' means the office of –

(a) Lord Justice of Appeal, Justice of the High Court or Circuit judge, in England and Wales;

(b) judge of the Court of Session or sheriff, in Scotland;

(c) Lord Justice of Appeal, judge of the High Court or county court judge, in Northern Ireland.

(2)   The holder of a judicial office may become a judge of the European Court of Human Rights ('the Court') without being required to relinquish his office.

(3)   But he is not required to perform the duties of his judicial office while he is a judge of the Court.

(4)   In respect of any period during which he is a judge of the Court –

(a) a Lord Justice of Appeal or Justice of the High Court is not to count as a judge of the relevant court for the purposes of section 2(1) or 4(1) of the Supreme Court Act 1981 (maximum number of judges) nor as a judge of the Supreme Court for the purposes of section 12(1) to (6) of that Act (salaries, etc);

(b) a judge of the Court of Session is not to count as a judge of that court for the purposes of section 1(1) of the Court of Session Act 1988 (maximum number of judges) or of section 9(1)(c) of the Administration of Justice Act 1973 ('the 1973 Act') (salaries, etc);

(c) a Lord Justice of Appeal or judge of the High Court in Northern Ireland is not to count as a judge of the relevant court for the purposes of section 2(1) or 3(1) of the Judicature (Northern Ireland) Act 1978 (maximum number of judges) nor as a judge of the Supreme Court of Northern Ireland for the purposes of section 9(1)(d) of the 1973 Act (salaries, etc);

(d) a Circuit judge is not to count as such for the purposes of section 18 of the Courts Act 1971 (salaries, etc);

(e) a sheriff is not to count as such for the purposes of section 14 of the Sheriff Courts (Scotland) Act 1907 (salaries, etc);

(f) a county court judge of Northern Ireland is not to count as such for the purposes of section 106 of the County Courts Act Northern Ireland) 1959 (salaries, etc).

(5)   If a sheriff principal is appointed a judge of the Court, section 11(1) of the Sheriff Courts (Scotland) Act 1971 (temporary appointment of sheriff principal) applies, while he holds that appointment, as if his office is vacant.

(6) Schedule 4 makes provision about judicial pensions in relation to the holder of a judicial office who serves as a judge of the Court.

(7) The Lord Chancellor or the Secretary of State may by order make such transitional provision (including, in particular, provision for a temporary increase in the maximum number of judges) as he considers appropriate in relation to any holder of a judicial office who has completed his service as a judge of the Court.

PARLIAMENTARY PROCEDURE

Statements of compatibility

19(1) A Minister of the Crown in charge of a Bill in either House of Parliament must, before Second Reading of the Bill –

(a) make a statement to the effect that in his view the provisions of the Bill are compatible with the Convention rights ('a statement of compatibility'); or

(b) make a statement to the effect that although he is unable to make a statement of compatibility the government nevertheless wishes the House to proceed with the Bill.

(2) The statement must be in writing and be published in such manner as the Minister making it considers appropriate.

SUPPLEMENTAL

Orders, etc, under this Act

20(1) Any power of a Minister of the Crown to make an order under this Act is exercisable by statutory instrument.

(2) The power of the Lord Chancellor or the Secretary of State to make rules (other than rules of court) under section 2(3) or 7(9) is exercisable by statutory instrument.

(3) Any statutory instrument made under section 14, 15 or 16(7) must be laid before Parliament.

(4) No order may be made by the Lord Chancellor or the Secretary of State under section 1(4), 7(11) or 16(2) unless a draft of the order has been laid before, and approved by, each House of Parliament.

(5) Any statutory instrument made under section 18(7) or Schedule 4, or to which subsection (2) applies, shall be subject to annulment in pursuance of a resolution of either House of Parliament.

(6) The power of a Northern Ireland department to make –

(a) rules under section 2(3)(c) or 7(9)(c), or

(b) an order under section 7(11),

is exercisable by statutory rule for the purposes of the Statutory Rules (Northern Ireland) Order 1979.

(7) Any rules made under section 2(3)(c) or 7(9)(c) shall be subject to negative resolution; and section 41(6) of the Interpretation Act Northern Ireland) 1954 (meaning of 'subject to negative resolution') shall apply as if the power to make the rules were conferred by an Act of the Northern Ireland Assembly.

(8)   No order may be made by a Northern Ireland department under section 7(11) unless a draft of the order has been laid before, and approved by, the Northern Ireland Assembly.

Interpretation, etc

21(1) In this Act –

'amend' includes repeal and apply (with or without modifications);

'the appropriate Minister' means the Minister of the Crown having charge of the appropriate authorised government department (within the meaning of the Crown Proceedings Act 1947);

'the Commission' means the European Commission of Human Rights;

'the Convention' means the Convention for the Protection of Human Rights and Fundamental Freedoms, agreed by the Council of Europe at Rome on 4th November 1950 as it has effect for the time being in relation to the United Kingdom;

'declaration of incompatibility' means a declaration under section 4;

'Minister of the Crown' has the same meaning as in the Ministers of the Crown Act 1975;

'Northern Ireland Minister' includes the First Minister and the deputy First Minister in Northern Ireland;

'primary legislation' means any –

(a)   public general Act;

(b)   local and personal Act;

(c)   private Act;

(d)   Measure of the Church Assembly;

(e)   Measure of the General Synod of the Church of England;

(f)   Order in Council –

   (i)   made in exercise of Her Majesty's Royal Prerogative;

   (ii) made under section 38(1)(a) of the Northern Ireland Constitution Act 1973 or the corresponding provision of the Northern Ireland Act 1998; or

   (iii) amending an Act of a kind mentioned in paragraph (a), (b) or (c); and includes an order or other instrument made under primary legislation (otherwise than by the National Assembly for Wales, a member of the Scottish Executive, a Northern Ireland Minister or a Northern Ireland department) to the extent to which it operates to bring one or more provisions of that legislation into force or amends any primary legislation;

'the First Protocol' means the protocol to the Convention agreed at Paris on 20th March 1952;

'the Sixth Protocol' means the protocol to the Convention agreed at Strasbourg on 28th April 1983;

'the Eleventh Protocol' means the protocol to the Convention (restructuring the control machinery established by the Convention) agreed at Strasbourg on 11th May 1994;

'remedial order' means an order under section 10;

'subordinate legislation' means any –

(a) Order in Council other than one –
   (i) made in exercise of Her Majesty's Royal Prerogative;
   (ii) made under section 38(1)(a) of the Northern Ireland Constitution Act 1973 or the corresponding provision of the Northern Ireland Act 1998; or
   (iii) amending an Act of a kind mentioned in the definition of primary legislation;
(b) Act of the Scottish Parliament;
(c) Act of the Parliament of Northern Ireland;
(d) Measure of the Assembly established under section 1 of the Northern Ireland Assembly Act 1973;
(e) Act of the Northern Ireland Assembly;
(f) order, rules, regulations, scheme, warrant, byelaw or other instrument made under primary legislation (except to the extent to which it operates to bring one or more provisions of that legislation into force or amends any primary legislation);
(g) order, rules, regulations, scheme, warrant, byelaw or other instrument made under legislation mentioned in paragraph (b), (c), (d) or (e) or made under an Order in Council applying only to Northern Ireland;
(h) order, rules, regulations, scheme, warrant, byelaw or other instrument made by a member of the Scottish Executive, a Northern Ireland Minister or a Northern Ireland department in exercise of prerogative or other executive functions of Her Majesty which are exercisable by such a person on behalf of Her Majesty;

'transferred matters' has the same meaning as in the Northern Ireland Act 1998; and

'tribunal' means any tribunal in which legal proceedings may be brought.

(2) The references in paragraphs (b) and (c) of section 2(1) to Articles are to Articles of the Convention as they had effect immediately before the coming into force of the Eleventh Protocol.

(3) The reference in paragraph (d) of section 2(1) to Article 46 includes a reference to Articles 32 and 54 of the Convention as they had effect immediately before the coming into force of the Eleventh Protocol.

(4) The references in section 2(1) to a report or decision of the Commission or a decision of the Committee of Ministers include references to a report or decision made as provided by paragraphs 3, 4 and 6 of Article 5 of the Eleventh Protocol (transitional provisions).

(5) Any liability under the Army Act 1955, the Air Force Act 1955 or the Naval Discipline Act 1957 to suffer death for an offence is replaced by a liability to imprisonment for life or any less punishment authorised by those Acts; and those Acts shall accordingly have effect with the necessary modifications.

Short title, commencement, application and extent

22(1) This Act may be cited as the Human Rights Act 1998.

(2) Sections 18, 20 and 21(5) and this section come into force on the passing of this Act.

(3) The other provisions of this Act come into force on such day as the Secretary of State may by order appoint; and different days may be appointed for different purposes.

(4) Paragraph (b) of subsection (1) of section 7 applies to proceedings brought by or at the instigation of a public authority whenever the act in question took place; but otherwise that subsection does not apply to an act taking place before the coming into force of that section.

(5) This Act binds the Crown.

(6) This Act extends to Northern Ireland.

(7) Section 21(5), so far as it relates to any provision contained in the Army Act 1955, the Air Force Act 1955 or the Naval Discipline Act 1957, extends to any place to which that provision extends.

SCHEDULE 1: THE ARTICLES

PART I: THE CONVENTION: RIGHTS AND FREEDOMS

Article 2: Right to life

1 Everyone's right to life shall be protected by law. No one shall be deprived of his life intentionally save in the execution of a sentence of a court following his conviction of a crime for which this penalty is provided by law.

2 Deprivation of life shall not be regarded as inflicted in contravention of this Article when it results from the use of force which is no more than absolutely necessary:
   (a) in defence of any person from unlawful violence;
   (b) in order to effect a lawful arrest or to prevent the escape of a person lawfully detained;
   (c) in action lawfully taken for the purpose of quelling a riot or insurrection.

Article 3: Prohibition of torture

No one shall be subjected to torture or to inhuman or degrading treatment or punishment.

Article 4: Prohibition of slavery and forced labour

1 No one shall be held in slavery or servitude.

2 No one shall be required to perform forced or compulsory labour.

3 For the purpose of this Article the term 'forced or compulsory labour' shall not include:
   (a) any work required to be done in the ordinary course of detention imposed according to the provisions of Article 5 of this Convention or during conditional release from such detention;
   (b) any service of a military character or, in case of conscientious objectors in countries where they are recognised, service exacted instead of compulsory military service;
   (c) any service exacted in case of an emergency or calamity threatening the life or well-being of the community;
   (d) any work or service which forms part of normal civic obligations.

Article 5: Right to liberty and security

1 Everyone has the right to liberty and security of person. No one shall be deprived of his liberty save in the following cases and in accordance with a procedure prescribed by law:

   (a) the lawful detention of a person after conviction by a competent court;

   (b) the lawful arrest or detention of a person for non-compliance with the lawful order of a court or in order to secure the fulfilment of any obligation prescribed by law;

   (c) the lawful arrest or detention of a person effected for the purpose of bringing him before the competent legal authority on reasonable suspicion of having committed an offence or when it is reasonably considered necessary to prevent his committing an offence or fleeing after having done so;

   (d) the detention of a minor by lawful order for the purpose of educational supervision or his lawful detention for the purpose of bringing him before the competent legal authority;

   (e) the lawful detention of persons for the prevention of the spreading of infectious diseases, of persons of unsound mind, alcoholics or drug addicts or vagrants;

   (f) the lawful arrest or detention of a person to prevent his effecting an unauthorised entry into the country or of a person against whom action is being taken with a view to deportation or extradition.

2 Everyone who is arrested shall be informed promptly, in a language which he understands, of the reasons for his arrest and of any charge against him.

3 Everyone arrested or detained in accordance with the provisions of paragraph 1(c) of this Article shall be brought promptly before a judge or other officer authorised by law to exercise judicial power and shall be entitled to trial within a reasonable time or to release pending trial. Release may be conditioned by guarantees to appear for trial.

4 Everyone who is deprived of his liberty by arrest or detention shall be entitled to take proceedings by which the lawfulness of his detention shall be decided speedily by a court and his release ordered if the detention is not lawful.

5 Everyone who has been the victim of arrest or detention in contravention of the provisions of this Article shall have an enforceable right to compensation.

Article 6: Right to a fair trial

1 In the determination of his civil rights and obligations or of any criminal charge against him, everyone is entitled to a fair and public hearing within a reasonable time by an independent and impartial tribunal established by law. Judgment shall be pronounced publicly but the press and public may be excluded from all or part of the trial in the interest of morals, public order or national security in a democratic society, where the interests of juveniles or the protection of the private life of the parties so require, or to the extent strictly necessary in the opinion of the court in special circumstances where publicity would prejudice the interests of justice.

2 Everyone charged with a criminal offence shall be presumed innocent until proved guilty according to law.

3   Everyone charged with a criminal offence has the following minimum rights:

(a) to be informed promptly, in a language which he understands and in detail, of the nature and cause of the accusation against him;

(b) to have adequate time and facilities for the preparation of his defence;

(c) to defend himself in person or through legal assistance of his own choosing or, if he has not sufficient means to pay for legal assistance, to be given it free when the interests of justice so require;

(d) to examine or have examined witnesses against him and to obtain the attendance and examination of witnesses on his behalf under the same conditions as witnesses against him;

(e) to have the free assistance of an interpreter if he cannot understand or speak the language used in court.

Article 7: No punishment without law

1   No one shall be held guilty of any criminal offence on account of any act or omission which did not constitute a criminal offence under national or international law at the time when it was committed. Nor shall a heavier penalty be imposed than the one that was applicable at the time the criminal offence was committed.

2   This Article shall not prejudice the trial and punishment of any person for any act or omission which, at the time when it was committed, was criminal according to the general principles of law recognised by civilised nations.

Article 8: Right to respect for private and family life

1   Everyone has the right to respect for his private and family life, his home and his correspondence.

2   There shall be no interference by a public authority with the exercise of this right except such as is in accordance with the law and is necessary in a democratic society in the interests of national security, public safety or the economic well-being of the country, for the prevention of disorder or crime, for the protection of health or morals, or for the protection of the rights and freedoms of others.

Article 9: Freedom of thought, conscience and religion

1   Everyone has the right to freedom of thought, conscience and religion; this right includes freedom to change his religion or belief and freedom, either alone or in community with others and in public or private, to manifest his religion or belief, in worship, teaching, practice and observance.

2   Freedom to manifest one's religion or beliefs shall be subject only to such limitations as are prescribed by law and are necessary in a democratic society in the interests of public safety, for the protection of public order, health or morals, or for the protection of the rights and freedoms of others.

Article 10: Freedom of expression

1   Everyone has the right to freedom of expression. This right shall include freedom to hold opinions and to receive and impart information and ideas without interference by public authority and regardless of frontiers. This

Article shall not prevent States from requiring the licensing of broadcasting, television or cinema enterprises.

2 The exercise of these freedoms, since it carries with it duties and responsibilities, may be subject to such formalities, conditions, restrictions or penalties as are prescribed by law and are necessary in a democratic society, in the interests of national security, territorial integrity or public safety, for the prevention of disorder or crime, for the protection of health or morals, for the protection of the reputation or rights of others, for preventing the disclosure of information received in confidence, or for maintaining the authority and impartiality of the judiciary.

Article 11: Freedom of assembly and association

1 Everyone has the right to freedom of peaceful assembly and to freedom of association with others, including the right to form and to join trade unions for the protection of his interests.

2 No restrictions shall be placed on the exercise of these rights other than such as are prescribed by law and are necessary in a democratic society in the interests of national security or public safety, for the prevention of disorder or crime, for the protection of health or morals or for the protection of the rights and freedoms of others. This Article shall not prevent the imposition of lawful restrictions on the exercise of these rights by members of the armed forces, of the police or of the administration of the State.

Article 12: Right to marry

Men and women of marriageable age have the right to marry and to found a family, according to the national laws governing the exercise of this right.

Article 14: Prohibition of discrimination

The enjoyment of the rights and freedoms set forth in this Convention shall be secured without discrimination on any ground such as sex, race, colour, language, religion, political or other opinion, national or social origin, association with a national minority, property, birth or other status.

Article 16: Restrictions on political activity of aliens

Nothing in Articles 10, 11 and 14 shall be regarded as preventing the High Contracting Parties from imposing restrictions on the political activity of aliens.

Article 17: Prohibition of abuse of rights

Nothing in this Convention may be interpreted as implying for any State, group or person any right to engage in any activity or perform any act aimed at the destruction of any of the rights and freedoms set forth herein or at their limitation to a greater extent than is provided for in the Convention.

Article 18: Limitation on use of restrictions on rights

The restrictions permitted under this Convention to the said rights and freedoms shall not be applied for any purpose other than those for which they have been prescribed.

PART II: THE FIRST PROTOCOL

Article 1: Protection of property
Every natural or legal person is entitled to the peaceful enjoyment of his possessions. No one shall be deprived of his possessions except in the public interest and subject to the conditions provided for by law and by the general principles of international law.

The preceding provisions shall not, however, in any way impair the right of a State to enforce such laws as it deems necessary to control the use of property in accordance with the general interest or to secure the payment of taxes or other contributions or penalties.

Article 2: Right to education
No person shall be denied the right to education. In the exercise of any functions which it assumes in relation to education and to teaching, the State shall respect the right of parents to ensure such education and teaching in conformity with their own religious and philosophical convictions.

Article 3: Right to free elections
The High Contracting Parties undertake to hold free elections at reasonable intervals by secret ballot, under conditions which will ensure the free expression of the opinion of the people in the choice of the legislature.

PART III: THE SIXTH PROTOCOL

Article 1: Abolition of the death penalty
The death penalty shall be abolished. No one shall be condemned to such penalty or executed.

Article 2: Death penalty in time of war
A State may make provision in its law for the death penalty in respect of acts committed in time of war or of imminent threat of war; such penalty shall be applied only in the instances laid down in the law and in accordance with its provisions. The State shall communicate to the Secretary General of the Council of Europe the relevant provisions of that law.

SCHEDULE 2: REMEDIAL ORDERS

Orders
1(1)   A remedial order may–
  (a) contain such incidental, supplemental, consequential or transitional provision as the person making it considers appropriate;
  (b) be made so as to have effect from a date earlier than that on which it is made;
  (c) make provision for the delegation of specific functions;
  (d) make different provision for different cases.

(2)   The power conferred by sub-paragraph (1)(a) includes–

(a)   power to amend primary legislation (including primary legislation other than that which contains the incompatible provision); and

(b)   power to amend or revoke subordinate legislation (including subordinate legislation other than that which contains the incompatible provision).

(3)   A remedial order may be made so as to have the same extent as the legislation which it affects.

(4)   No person is to be guilty of an offence solely as a result of the retrospective effect of a remedial order.

Procedure

2   No remedial order may be made unless–

(a)   a draft of the order has been approved by a resolution of each House of Parliament made after the end of the period of 60 days beginning with the day on which the draft was laid; or

(b)   it is declared in the order that it appears to the person making it that, because of the urgency of the matter, it is necessary to make the order without a draft being so approved.

Orders laid in draft

3(1)   No draft may be laid under paragraph 2(a) unless–

(a)   the person proposing to make the order has laid before Parliament a document which contains a draft of the proposed order and the required information; and

(b)   the period of 60 days, beginning with the day on which the document required by this sub-paragraph was laid, has ended.

(2)   If representations have been made during that period, the draft laid under paragraph 2(a) must be accompanied by a statement containing–

(a)   a summary of the representations; and

(b)   if, as a result of the representations, the proposed order has been changed, details of the changes.

Urgent cases

4(1)   If a remedial order ('the original order') is made without being approved in draft, the person making it must lay it before Parliament, accompanied by the required information, after it is made.

(2)   If representations have been made during the period of 60 days beginning with the day on which the original order was made, the person making it must (after the end of that period) lay before Parliament a statement containing–

(a)   a summary of the representations; and

(b)   if, as a result of the representations, he considers it appropriate to make changes to the original order, details of the changes.

(3)   If sub-paragraph (2)(b) applies, the person making the statement must–

(a)   make a further remedial order replacing the original order; and

(b)   lay the replacement order before Parliament.

(4)   If, at the end of the period of 120 days beginning with the day on which the original order was made, a resolution has not been passed by each House approving the original or replacement order, the order ceases to have effect (but without that affecting anything previously done under either order or the power to make a fresh remedial order).

Definitions

5   In this Schedule–

'representations' means representations about a remedial order (or proposed remedial order) made to the person making (or proposing to make) it and includes any relevant Parliamentary report or resolution; and

'required information' means–

(a)   an explanation of the incompatibility which the order (or proposed order) seeks to remove, including particulars of the relevant declaration, finding or order; and

(b)   a statement of the reasons for proceeding under section 10 and for making an order in those terms.

Calculating periods

6   In calculating any period for the purposes of this Schedule, no account is to be taken of any time during which–

(a)   Parliament is dissolved or prorogued; or

(b)   both Houses are adjourned for more than four days.

7(1)   This paragraph applies in relation to–

(a)   any remedial order made, and any draft of such an order proposed to be made–

(i)   by the Scottish Ministers; or

(ii)   within devolved competence (within the meaning of the Scotland Act 1998) by Her Majesty in Council; and

(b)   any document or statement to be laid in connection with such an order (or proposed order).

(2)   This Schedule has effect in relation to any such order (or proposed order), document or statement subject to the following modifications.

(3)   Any reference to Parliament, each House of Parliament or both Houses of Parliament shall be construed as a reference to the Scottish Parliament.

(4)   Paragraph 6 does not apply and instead, in calculating any period for the purposes of this Schedule, no account is to be taken of any time during which the Scottish Parliament is dissolved or is in recess for more than four days.

SCHEDULE 3: RESERVATION

[PART I: DEROGATION repealed by SI 2001 No 1216]

PART II: RESERVATION

At the time of signing the present (First) Protocol, I declare that, in view of certain provisions of the Education Acts in the United Kingdom, the principle affirmed in the second sentence of Article 2 is accepted by the United Kingdom only so far as it is compatible with the provision of efficient instruction and training, and the avoidance of unreasonable public expenditure.

Dated 20 March 1952. Made by the United Kingdom Permanent Representative to the Council of Europe.

SCHEDULE 4: JUDICIAL PENSIONS

Duty to make orders about pensions

1(1) The appropriate Minister must by order make provision with respect to pensions payable to or in respect of any holder of a judicial office who serves as an ECHR judge.

(2) A pensions order must include such provision as the Minister making it considers is necessary to secure that–

(a) an ECHR judge who was, immediately before his appointment as an ECHR judge, a member of a judicial pension scheme is entitled to remain as a member of that scheme;

(b) the terms on which he remains a member of the scheme are those which would have been applicable had he not been appointed as an ECHR judge; and

(c) entitlement to benefits payable in accordance with the scheme continues to be determined as if, while serving as an ECHR judge, his salary was that which would (but for section 18(4)) have been payable to him in respect of his continuing service as the holder of his judicial office.

Contributions

2 A pensions order may, in particular, make provision–

(a) for any contributions which are payable by a person who remains a member of a scheme as a result of the order, and which would otherwise be payable by deduction from his salary, to be made otherwise than by deduction from his salary as an ECHR judge; and

(b) for such contributions to be collected in such manner as may be determined by the administrators of the scheme.

Amendments of other enactments

3 A pensions order may amend any provision of, or made under, a pensions Act in such manner and to such extent as the Minister making the order considers necessary or expedient to ensure the proper administration of any scheme to which it relates.

Definitions

4   In this Schedule–

'appropriate Minister' means–

(a) in relation to any judicial office whose jurisdiction is exercisable exclusively in relation to Scotland, the Secretary of State; and

(b) otherwise, the Lord Chancellor;

'ECHR judge' means the holder of a judicial office who is serving as a judge of the Court;

'judicial pension scheme' means a scheme established by and in accordance with a pensions Act;

'pensions Act' means–

(a) the County Courts Act Northern Ireland) 1959;

(b) the Sheriffs' Pensions (Scotland) Act 1961;

(c) the Judicial Pensions Act 1981; or

(d) the Judicial Pensions and Retirement Act 1993; and

'pensions order' means an order made under paragraph 1.

Index